English for Academic Rese

Series Editor
Adrian Wallwork, English for Academics SAS
Pisa, Italy

This series aims to help non-native, English-speaking researchers communicate in English. The books are designed like manuals or user guides to help readers find relevant information quickly, and assimilate it rapidly and effectively.

More information about this series at https://link.springer.com/bookseries/13913

Adrian Wallwork

Writing an Academic Paper in English

Intermediate Level

 Springer

Adrian Wallwork
English for Academics
Pisa, Italy

ISSN 2625-3445   ISSN 2625-3453 (electronic)
English for Academic Research
ISBN 978-3-030-95614-1   ISBN 978-3-030-95615-8 (eBook)
https://doi.org/10.1007/978-3-030-95615-8

This Springer imprint is published by the registered company Springer Nature Switzerland AG
The registered company address is: Gewerbestrasse 11, 6330 Cham, Switzerland

Introduction

WHO FOR
- Students of academic English (PhD students, postdocs, undergraduates)
- Teachers of English for Academic Purposes (EAP)

ENGLISH LEVEL
Minimum level: mid to upper-intermediate (CEFR level: B2), but can also be used with advanced students (CEFR levels: C1, C2).

If used as a coursebook, the class can consist of students with different levels of English. However, ideally they should all be at the same point in their university curriculum (e.g. all undergraduates or all first-year PhD students).

TYPE AND COVERAGE
Course on academic English (EAP) and/or self-study guide for students.

The book covers the typical skills to write the various sections of an academic paper for publication in a journal. However, the skills learned can be used not only by PhD students and postdocs, but also by undergraduates to write essays, reports, and theses.

STRUCTURE OF BOOK
After an introduction (Chapter 1) on the importance of communication in academia, Chapters 2–10 cover the various sections of a paper: Introduction, Methods, Results, Discussion, Conclusions, Abstract. The final chapter (Chapter 11) summarizes the entire book and gives ideas on further exercises for improving the skills learned in this book.

PRONOUNS
This book uses the generic pronouns *they* and *their*, rather than *he/she* and *his/her*.

Contents

Chapter 1
Getting started

1.1 What skills do I need to be an academic?

1. What skills do you need to be an academic today?

2. Are these skills different from those of 20–30 years ago? If so, how?

3. What skills do you already have? Which ones do you think you still need to learn? Why?

4. How important is it for you to publish papers? How will your publications impact on your career?

Some academics tend to be highly competitive, non-collaborative (i.e. not very interested in sharing results), and focused on publishing or presenting as many papers as possible (i.e. bibliometric indicators). Other aspects of academic life, such as teaching and solving the problems of society, are given low priority as they are considered as being unproductive because they don't further an academic's career.

However, there is also a trend towards more open science and more open data infrastructures. Thus it is now considered important to conduct research that

- enables others to collaborate and contribute

- encourages the free availability of data, procedures, protocols etc, so that results can be replicated, re-used and redistributed

- has a clear goal, i.e. is mission-oriented

- will benefit society in general, i.e. will not just be of interest to a small group of researchers

© The Author(s), under exclusive license to Springer Nature
Switzerland AG 2022
A. Wallwork, *Writing an Academic Paper in English*, English for Academic
Research, https://doi.org/10.1007/978-3-030-95615-8_1

1.1   What skills do I need to be an academic? (cont.)

This means that you will need to learn more about how to communicate your results clearly and to collaborate with others. Such communication skills involve:

- being open-minded and flexible, with an ability to debate constructively
- developing relationships with your local community and with the community of scientists
- coordinating projects

Obviously, you still need to show excellence and rigor in your research. However, no matter how good your results are, if you cannot communicate them well (orally or written), they will have little real value. If you want a successful and rewarding career you need to learn to write well – and this book will teach you how!

If you see yourself not just as an academic, but also as someone who wants to help society by providing new solutions through your research, I think you will write more clearly.

1.2   What writing skills do I need to learn before writing my first paper?

1) Approximately how many research papers are published per year?

   a) 2,500 b) 25,000 c) 250,000 d) 2,500,000

2) Thomson Reuter's Web of Science holds 58 million items. What percentage of these papers do you think have never been cited or only cited once? [Cited = mentioned in another author's paper]

   a) 10% b) 25% c) 50% d) 75%

3) Which THREE the following kinds of mistake do you think are most likely to cause a reviewer of your paper to require 'major revision' due to 'poor English'?

   a) 5–10 grammar mistakes

   b) 5–10 vocabulary mistakes

   c) 5–10 very long complex sentences that are difficult to understand on the first reading

   d) 5–10 vague words or phrases where precision is required

   e) 3–5 ambiguous sentences (e.g. where it is not clear what *it, they, this, the former* and other pronouns refer to) and sentences where the word order does not reflect the usual subject-verb-object of English

   f) 3–5 spelling mistakes

   g) findings that are not highlighted and whose novelty is not explained

   h) lack of clarity regarding who obtained particular results: the author of the paper or the author of another paper

   i) main contribution not clear

   j) plagiarism (i.e. where you have copied word for word from a previous paper, either someone else's or even a previous paper that you or your research group has published)

   k) redundancy – words, phrases, sentences and paragraphs that add no value for the reader, but simply make the paper much longer

1.2 What writing skills do I need to learn before writing my first paper? (cont.)

1) d

2) c (Only 14,499 papers have more than 1,000 citations).

Source of statistics: https://www.nature.com/news/the-top-100-papers-1.16224.

3)

a) b) f) Grammar, vocabulary and spelling are unlikely to require a 'major' revision, only a 'minor' revision. This is because these kinds of errors do not usually prevent the reader from understanding the meaning of what you are saying. However, just one spelling mistake may be enough to catch the reviewer's eye and make him/her ask for a 'minor revision'. Remember that any kind of revision delays your paper being published.

c) d) e) h) k) These are all readability issues – they stop the reader from <u>immediately</u> understanding what you are saying. They may force the reader to read the sentence several times before they can understand the meaning. These, in my opinion, merit a major revision. In any case, even if the reviewer doesn't mention them, they will certainly impact on the number of readers who cite your paper – if readers can't understand what you are saying, they are unlikely to mention your paper in their paper. Redundancy is a big problem in many academic papers: e.g. using three words where one is enough. Redundancy does not stop the reader from understanding, but it might simply make them want to stop reading the paper as the mental effort and time required is too much/long. Readability issues are often mentioned by native English-speaking reviewers, who, on the other hand, are often more tolerant than non-natives regarding grammar mistakes.

g) and i) These will almost certainly lead to a request for a major review, or the paper may simply be rejected.

j) If you copy entire phrases from other papers (even your own papers) this is considered unacceptable. In fact, many journals use software to check for this issue. However, many reviewers will not even notice. My advice is to learn how to paraphrase, and also to always remember to cite the author whose sentence you are paraphrasing. A lot of plagiarism will undermine your credibility and may lead to a paper being rejected.

1.3 What do I need to think about before I start planning my paper?

1. Which is more important: a) doing you research? b) writing the paper that describes your research?

2. What areas of life do you make plans for? Choose one or two of the items below (a–e). Decide i) how long in advance you start to make plans and what these plans consist of, ii) whether it is possible to make no plans at all, and what happens if you don't make plans.

   a) buying a car, a house

   b) exams

   c) holidays

   d) job interviews

   e) weddings

1) If you don't write the paper, the world will not know about the research you've done. But simply writing a paper is not enough. The paper has to be clear and accurate, and must be easy to understand. To write such a paper, you need to plan it carefully.

2) To write a well-structured paper in good clear English, you need to have a method. If you don't have a good method you may waste a lot of time having to re-plan and re-write entire sections of your paper.

Write notes about:

- why you want to write a paper and publish your research

- what you can do to ensure that you write a good paper – what steps you need to follow

- how you will choose a journal

- the numbers of weeks/months you think it will take you to complete your paper (then consider doubling the number!)

- the advantages of writing each section i) in a separate file or one big file, ii) simultaneously or one at a time, iii) in the order in which they will actually appear in the paper (e.g. Abstract first, Conclusions last) or in order of easiness (typically the Methods is the easiest)

1.4 What questions do I need to think about before I write my first paper or do my first presentation of my research?

1. Why did you choose your specific research topic – think about what it says about: i) your interests / ambitions when you were younger, ii) how it fits your personality, iii) how it follows on from your previous studies

2. Why is your research important to you ? Why do you find it interesting?

3. Why is it important to tell other people about your research? If no one knew about it, what would happen?

4. What would happen if NO ONE did the research that are you doing? Why is it vital that researchers are carrying out studies in your specific field?

5. Do you think public money should be used to fund your research? In what ways could your research benefit society?

Before you start writing you need to have a very clear idea of:

- what your research goal was
- what your most important findings are and how you can demonstrate that they are true
- how these findings differ from, and add to, previous knowledge
- what new knowledge you are adding to science

You know implicitly what the importance of your findings are – after all, you may have been working for months and years on the project.

But the reader does not know.

You must give the reader a clear message.

1.4 What questions do I need to think about before I write my first paper or do my first presentation of my research? (cont.)

Chat about your research with a friend or member of your family. This will help you to understand what is and is not important about your methodology and findings. After you have had this chat with a few different groups of people, write some notes down about what you said under the section headings: Abstract, Introduction, Methods, Results, Discussion.

Under each heading try to think how you can highlight the importance of your research, how it adds value to previous research in your field, and think about what your results really mean.

Using these notes, give an oral presentation of your methods and results to your colleagues. These colleagues can then give you useful comments and criticisms. They may be able to give you alternative interpretations, help you understand your anomalous findings, reassure you that it is OK to include your negative findings, and bring to your attention anything that you may have missed out.

1.5   How important are the journal's *Instructions for Authors*?

Before you begin writing your paper, you need to choose the most appropriate journal to publish it in. Your professor and colleagues can help you with this decision. See 1.3 in *English for Writing Research Papers*.

When you have chosen your journal, download the *Instructions for Authors* from the journal's website page.

On the next page is an extract from the Instructions to Authors from *The American Veterinary Medical Association,* which is a semi-monthly, peer-reviewed, general veterinary medical journal owned by The American Veterinary Medical Association, and is reproduced with their kind permission.

The full document can be found here:

https://www.avma.org/sites/default/files/resources/javma-ifa.pdf

1.5 How important are the journal's *Instructions for Authors* (cont.)

The text for an Original Study begins with an introduction (which does not have a heading) and then is organized under the following headings:

- Materials and Methods

- Results

- Discussion

The **Introduction** should supply sufficient pertinent background information to allow readers to understand why the study was performed. It must include a rationale for the study, a clear statement of the purpose of the study, and the investigators' hypothesis or hypotheses. The introduction is not intended to be a thorough review of the published literature on a subject. Rather, it should be brief (often, 2 or 3 paragraphs will suffice) and should focus on identifying the specific problem the study is meant to address; describing how the study addresses the problem, differs from previous studies, or improves our understanding; and explaining what the present study was meant to do and what hypotheses it was meant to test.

The **Materials and Methods** section should describe the study design in sufficient detail to allow others to re-produce the study. A subsection detailing statistical methods used to summarize data, evaluate data distributions, and test hypotheses, along with a statement regarding the cutoff for significance used for hypothesis testing, should be provided.

Appendices and methods-related **figures** should be cited parenthetically. Products (including soft-ware), equipment, and drugs.

should be identified in the text by chemical or generic names or descriptions. For all statistical tests, authors are required to indicate whether applicable test assumptions were met

When citing **software products**, a footnote should be used to cite the software (eg, PROC GLM, SAS, version 9.2, SAS Institute Inc, Cary, NC) and a reference should be used to cite a user's guide (eg, SAS/STAT 9.2 user's guide. Cary, NC: SAS Institute Inc, 2008;page number).

The **Results** section should provide data that are clearly and simply stated without discussion or conclusions. Tables and figures should be cited parenthetically. Authors should refrain from repeating within the text data that are also presented in tables and figures and are encouraged to report the number of subjects included in any statistical calculations (eg, means, medians, and results of statistical tests), particularly if that number differs among described variables.

The **Discussion** section should focus on findings in the manuscript and should be brief (generally no more than 2,000 words), containing only discussion that is necessary for the interpretation of findings. The major findings, including whether hypotheses stated in the introduction were supported, should be given in the first paragraph. Strengths and weaknesses of the study should be acknowledged, and the discussion should end with the principal points that readers should take away. The Discussion section should concentrate mainly on what is known in non-human animals, with less emphasis on what is known in humans. It should not contain any subheadings.

1.5   How important are the journal's *Instructions for Authors* (cont.)

The *Instructions to Authors* on the previous page highlight that:

- There are very precise requirements on how to write each section.
- The Introduction may only consist of 2 or 3 paragraphs. Also the Discussion is relatively brief.
- The purpose of the Materials & Methods is to enable readers to re-produce the study.
- The Results section should provide data that are clearly and simply stated without discussion or conclusions.
- This journal has its own specific style guide that governs how, for instance, you report appendices, tables, figures, and software.

Note that the *Instructions to Authors* of other journals may differ considerably, for example with much longer Introductions and Discussions, and also a Conclusions section may be required. Ensure that you follow the instructions carefully. If you don't, you may find that your paper is initially rejected because it does not conform to the requirements of the journal.

The *Instructions for Authors* tell you how to organize and format your paper, and whether there might be more suitable forms of publication for your research e.g. a letter, a case study, book chapter.

One of the most prestigious journals in the world is the British Medical Journal (BMJ). The BMJ's Instructions for Authors contain useful advice about various topics.

1. Whether the BMJ is the right journal for your research article.

   https://www.bmj.com/about-bmj/resources-authors/bmj-right-journal-my-research-article

2. How to write a paper. You can download a pdf entitled 'BMJ Guidance for Authors'. This is a dense document, but the most important information in terms of how to write a scientific paper can be found on page 5 (what to include in the Discussion), and page 6 which tells you how to write the cover letter.

   https://www.bmj.com/about-bmj/resources-authors/article-types

1.5 How important are the journal's *Instructions for Authors* (cont.)

3. You can find details about the BMJ's house style – these are rules regarding, for example, punctuation, grammar and spelling.

   https://www.bmj.com/about-bmj/resources-authors/house-style

Below are some examples of BMJ recommendations.

a) Write in the active and use the first person (*we*) where necessary.

b) Try to avoid long sentences that have several embedded clauses.

c) Use commas before "and" and "or" in lists.

d) Sex: avoid "he" as a general pronoun. Make the nouns (and pronouns) plural, then use "they"; if that's not possible, use "he or she".

e) Minimal capitalisation. Use capitals only for names and proper nouns.

1.6   What is the best order to write the sections of my paper?

Which of the following do you think is the best order to write a paper in?

1. title – abstract – introduction etc

2. introduction, methods, results, discussion, abstract, title

3. methods, results, discussion / introduction, abstract, title

There is no standard order in which you should write the various sections of your paper. You should choose the order that suits you best. This may involve writing several sections simultaneously.

Many authors start with the Methods. This is generally the easiest section to write because this is the part that will usually be clearest in your mind. Beginning with the Methods will also give you the confidence and impetus you need to move on to the other sections of the paper.

However, it may be best to start with the Abstract as this will help you to focus on identifying the key aspects of your research. You will certainly need to revisit / rewrite the Abstract when you have finished writing the actual paper.

You might find it useful to look at the scientific study protocol that you wrote when you outlined the aims of your research at the beginning of your PhD or before you began your current project. Here you should have written out your goals very clearly, and this will help you to write your Abstract.

The hardest part for most authors is the Discussion, where you have to interpret your results and compare them with other authors' results. While you are writing the Discussion, you may find it useful to draft the Introduction, as some of the authors you mention will appear both in the Introduction and the Discussion.

A possible order for writing the various sections is thus:

> Abstract (very rough draft)
>
> Methods
>
> Results
>
> Discussion
>
> Introduction
>
> Conclusions
>
> Abstract (final version)
>
> Title

1.7   How important is it to analyse other papers in my field? What will I learn?

Choose some papers that are frequently cited in your field of research and that you will probably use in the Introduction and/or Discussion of your paper. 'Cited' means that other authors refer to these papers when talking about their own work.

Write notes using some or all of the following headings:

- problem that the research addresses

- background information

- aspects that highlight that the research is innovative

- method used and the steps the author carried out

- materials, equipment and software used

- results achieved

- analysis and interpretation of these results

- strengths and weaknesses of the research

- implications for further research

This analysis should help you to:

1. write your own literature review, because through your review you will be very familiar with what has and has not been investigated, and where your research might fit in with what is already known and the current state of the art

2. identify the differences in other researchers' approaches and results compared to your research

3. note down the strengths and weaknesses (including possibly bias) in the work of others

These three points should enable you to understand in what ways your research is unique, innovative, interesting and useful, and how it extends what is already in the literature. Your aim is to find a knowledge gap to fill.

1.7 How important is it to analyse other papers in my field? What will I learn? (cont.)

As you read your model papers, note down English phrases that the author uses and which you think might be useful for your paper. Such phrases will help to increase the readability of your text, as they will be familiar to your readers.

Each chapter in this book, apart from this chapter, contains a list of Useful Phrases (see the index of Useful Phrases on page 191) which you can use in the various sections of your paper.

You should try to add new phrases that you find to these lists.

1.8 Do's and Don'ts of preparation

DO write notes in English throughout your research project. This means that you will already have much of the content you need when you finally start writing your manuscript. It also means that you will get a lot of practice in writing in English and it may also help you to discover any gaps in your understanding of your topic.

DO write your paper with the referees in mind. They are the ones that decide whether your paper will be published.

DON'T make the referees' job harder than it needs to be. Referees review manuscripts in their own time and have no direct financial reward for doing so. So do everything you can to make the referee's work easier and more pleasurable – clear English, clear layout, clear tables etc. By doing so you will increase the chances of your paper being accepted.

DO pay close attention to your English. It is possible to write a paper in completely accurate English, but still have a paper rejected for poor writing skills – which is what happens even to native English researchers. On the other hand, a paper that is constructed well, and is easy to read, may be accepted (perhaps with some requests for minor revisions) even if the English is not totally accurate. All referees will appreciate it if you use simple language.

DO set the language to US or UK English before you start writing the document. Enable the spelling and grammar check. This means that as you are writing, Microsoft Word (or equivalent) will automatically highlight spelling mistakes and potential grammar mistakes. For a free download on how to use Microsoft Word's automatic spell check and Editor function, see e4ac.com/resources. To learn some spelling rules and typical mistakes that automatic spell checkers don't always find see 2.5 in *Grammar, Usage and Strategies in Academic English*.

DON'T automatically discount the idea of using automatic translation, particularly if your native language is commonly spoken. So, consider writing the paper in your own language and then using an automatic translator (e.g. Google Translate). For a free download on how to use Google Translate with surprisingly accurate results, see e4ac.com/resources.

1.9 Exercises

Choose one paper that is close to your topic, preferably from the journal where you intend to publish your paper. The paper should be by a native English speaker, and be one that you find easy and enjoyable to read.

Notice how your model paper is structured:

- how does the author begin?
- what points do they make in each section?
- how do they link paragraphs together?
- how do they connect the Results with the Discussion?
- how do they present the Conclusions?

Write a few lines to answer each of the questions below.

1. what problem are you trying to solve / investigate?
2. how did you solve / investigate it?
3. how does your solution / investigation differ from previous approaches?
4. what did you discover?
5. how do your findings differ from what is already in the literature, and what do they mean?

English for Writing Research Papers

Chapters 1–8, and 11 on planning & preparation, word order, dividing up long sentences, removing redundancy, avoiding ambiguity, clarifying what you did (rather than other authors), highlighting your findings, plagiarism & paraphrasing.

Chapter 2
Introduction and Review of the Literature

2.1 What is an Introduction?

Which of these questions below

- can you answer in relation to your research topic?
- do you think you should mention in the Introduction to your paper?

1. When did research in your area first begin?
2. What problem were the pioneers (i.e. the first investigators) trying to solve?
3. Which scientists/authors/research groups questioned / extended the pioneers' theories and results?
4. What is the state-of-the-art today?
5. What areas still need investigating and why?
6. What is the purpose of your own particular research?
7. How does your research fit in with what has already been done?
8. What gap does it fill?
9. What are the long-term goals of researchers in your area? At what point do you think (hope) research in your field will be in ten, twenty, thirty years' time?

When you write your introduction to your paper, imagine you are writing for your fellow students. Only tell them what THEY need to know. You are NOT writing a general introduction to your research field. Instead you are writing an introduction to YOUR SPECIFIC STUDY. This is particularly true for pure sciences and medicine, where readers who are probably up to date with your research area and thus want to read new information rather than background details. So, you really only need to answer questions 4–8.

On the other hand, the length of an Introduction and the amount of detail given is much greater in subjects such as political / social sciences, economics and the humanities in general.

© The Author(s), under exclusive license to Springer Nature
Switzerland AG 2022
A. Wallwork, *Writing an Academic Paper in English*, English for Academic
Research, https://doi.org/10.1007/978-3-030-95615-8_2

2.1   What is an Introduction? (cont.)

Look at Introductions in published papers in your field and check:

- how long they are
- how they are structured
- whether you are required to have a very strong theoretical framework for your study

In any case, ensure that:

- you mention the state of the art (i.e. the current trends in your field)
- it is clear for the reader why you have mentioned a particular previous paper
- any papers you mention in the Introduction are also mentioned in the Bibliography, and vice versa.

2.2 What is the purpose of my Introduction?

Let's imagine that your research has been on X.

When you began your research on X, you had an aim. In order to achieve this aim you found a method.

With that method you produced some results.

With these results you probably either proved something, disproved something, or found nothing conclusive.

The purpose of the Introduction is to help the reader understand:

1. what problem you are trying to resolve or what your research question is

2. what other research on X has been done, why it was done, and what it proved.

3. how your research on X fits in with the previous research, and what your research adds to our knowledge of X.

Step 1 requires you to review the literature, i.e. analyze what other authors in your field have done. This does NOT entail giving the reader the complete history of your field, but only those very specific parts of the history that relate to the work described in your paper.

Step 2 requires you to use the information you have provided in Step 1 to explain your own motivations for carrying out your research.

Imagine you are explaining your research to a friend or member of the family. Complete the sentences below using simple everyday language. You can modify the sentences where appropriate.

In my research I am investigating ___

I am doing this investigation because I am trying to resolve a general problem regarding ___

So far, other researchers in my field have done ___

However, they have not done ___

The fact that other researchers have not done x is a problem because ___

So my solution is ___

2.2 What is the purpose of my Introduction? (cont.)

In disciplines such as medicine, biology, chemistry, physics, computer science, and engineering, an Introduction is NOT structured by first presenting Step 1 and then presenting Step 2, and then moving on to the Methods section. Instead, the structure is a whole series of Step 1 + 2, Step 1 + Step 2 etc. This structure is explained in the next subsection.

2.3 What should be my aims when reviewing the literature?

Much of your Introduction will be devoted to reviewing the literature in your field of research. Alternatively, your journal may require you to review the literature in a dedicated section called 'Review of the Literature' or 'State of the Art'.

In order to review this literature, it helps to think in terms of i) the pros and cons (i.e. the advantages and drawbacks) of previous studies, and ii) the gap that needs to be filled (i.e. what work still needs to be done).

Think about your life now as a student: the good things, the bad things, what you would like to change and how (solutions). Complete the following table with three or more items per column.

POSITIVE THINGS	NEGATIVE THINGS	SOLUTIONS

Now write a short text in which you connect the three areas (positive, negative, improvements) in a logical way. You may need words and phrases such as the ones below:

thus, consequently, and so, this means that (8.9)

in addition, also, moreover (8.2)

instead, on the other hand (8.8)

however, but, despite this (8.7)

even though, even if (8.5)

Note that the numbers in brackets are links to another book in this series entitled *Grammar, Usage and Strategies*, which explains how these words and phrases are used. By doing this exercise you will learn a key skill in writing Introductions: helping the reader see the connections between the research that has been done in your field, and what the consequences of this research have been.

2.4 What structure should I use when reviewing the literature?

Before you started your research on X, you probably looked at the literature on X. Let's imagine now that you are writing the review of the literature and that you have selected 12 studies that are similar to your study, or in some way inspired your research.

If you can, separate these 12 studies into smaller groups, for example three groups of four studies, or two groups of five studies and one group of two. These groups should contain papers that are in some way more similar to each other than to the papers in the other groups.

First create a table, similar to the one below:

Authors in Group 1	What they did	Pros / Progress made	Cons / Limitations / Gap still to fill	Your solution
Pallino et al. (2023)	New method	Positive results for x, y and z.	Small sample size	Much larger sample
Smith et al. (2024)	Extends previous research on P, Q and R.	New insights into P and Q	Inconclusive results regarding R.	Conclusive results regarding R.
etc.				
Authors in Group 2	**What they did**	**Pros / Progress made**	**Cons / Limitations / Gap still to fill**	**Your solution**
Chang et al. (2023)	Totally different approach to X.	Rigorous and innovative method	Approach inappropriate for X.	Appropriate approach for X.
etc.				

On the basis of your table, complete steps 1–4 below.

Under each step below are typical phrases used when writing the review of the literature

1. INTRODUCE GROUP 1.

    Three main studies have approached the problem of X by doing Y.

    Smith et al. (2022) used Y to stabilize the elements of X. Blah blah blah (*details on their method*).

    Li et al. (2023) used Y to increase the volume of X. Blah blah blah (*details on their method*).

    Mitterand et al. (2024) used Y to ...

2.4 What structure should I use when reviewing the literature? (cont.)

2. TELL THE READER ABOUT THE PROGRESS MADE BY THESE THREE STUDIES.

   Their results led to ... enabled ...

3. EXPLAIN WHAT THE THREE STUDIES DID NOT DO OR FAILED TO DO.

   However, their results were inconclusive because ...

4. BRIEFLY DESCRIBE WHAT YOU DID TO SOLVE THE PROBLEMS THAT THE THREE PREVIOUS STUDIES WERE UNABLE TO SOLVE.

   In our study, we solved the problem of X by doing Z.

5. INTRODUCE GROUP 2, AND REPEAT THE SAME STRUCTURE AS YOU USED FOR GROUP 1.

The result of this structure (i.e. Steps 1–5 above) is that the reader will then be very clear about:

- the background to your research field
- what other researchers before you have done and what they achieved
- why you wanted to do what you did, i.e. what your research question is
- how what you did fits in with what has already been done

Ensure that you dedicate a **separate** paragraph (or more than one paragraph if you have a lot to say) to each group of authors that have a similar approach to each other or who encountered similar difficulties.

Begin a **new paragraph** talking about how your approach aims to **solve the cons** that you have discussed in the previous paragraph, or how your study **builds in an orginal way** on previous studies.

At the end of the review of the literature, write one paragraph summarizing the aims of your paper and your method. In one sentence, highlight why your research is important.

2.5 Model 1 – general sciences: Introduction starting with definition, state of the art, problem to resolve

> If you are not studying sciences (i.e. you are a humanities student) do NOT do this exercise, instead do the exercises in 3.1 or 3.2. Your choice of 3.1 or 3.2 will depend on how Introductions tend to be written in your chosen journal.

Imagine your research area is telephone batteries. You could begin your Introduction with one or more of these four points.

Note: If your particular area of research does not require Points 1 and/or 2, start directly with 3 and 4.

	FUNCTION	AUTHOR'S TEXT
1	**definition of your topic (batteries) plus background**	An XYZ battery is a battery that ... The electrodes in an XYZ telephone battery are made of a composite of gold and silver, coated with a layer of platinum. The gold and silver provide structural support, while the platinum provides resilience.
2	**accepted state of the art + problem to be resolved**	The performance of the battery can be strongly affected by the number of times the battery is recharged and the duration of each individual recharge. The battery is subject to three possible failure modes. ...
3	**your objectives**	A research program has recently been started by the authors in collaboration with a major battery manufacturer, with the goal of developing new design models for XYZ batteries. Analytical techniques are needed that can predict ...
4	**introduction to the literature** on batteries	Computational techniques have been extensively applied to the study of the lifetime of XYZ batteries, in particular with regard to the number of times a battery is charged. However, little research to date has focused on the length of each individual recharge.

2.5 Model 1 – general sciences: Introduction starting with definition, state of the art, problem to resolve (cont.)

5	**survey of relevant literature.** NOTE: This may be a separate section of the paper (see 2.4).	More recent research has occurred in the field of laptop and jPud batteries. Evans [15] studied the lifetime in 5G jPud batteries. Smith [16] and Jones [18] found that ... However their findings failed to account for ...
6	**what is missing in the state-of-the-art, i.e. the gap you aim to fill**	To the best of our knowledge there are no results in the literature regarding how the length of each recharge impacts on the silver and gold in the electrodes.
7	**aim of your paper**	The aim of the present work is to construct a model to perform a comprehensive investigation of the effect of recharging on the electrodes, and to find a new proportion in the number of metals used. The assumptions of Smith [16] and Jones [18] are used as a starting point. ... We believe that this is the first time that electrodes have been investigated from the point of view of ...
8	**your main results / conclusions**	The results of the model show that ...

The last part of many Introductions is an explanation for the reader of how the paper is structured. To learn how to write this explanation, see 3.6 (Useful Phrases).

Use points 1–8 above as the basis for writing your own Introduction. For the purposes of this exercise, if you don't have time to do the review of the literature (or you already did the exercise in 2.4) – then don't do point 5.

For a detailed analysis of the points 1–8 above, see 14.5–14.7 in *English for Writing Research Papers*.

2.6   What tenses are typically used in an Introduction and in the Review of the Literature?

The tenses shown below appear in the order that they would normally be used in an Introduction.

PRESENT SIMPLE: general background, i.e. what is known already.

> An XYZ battery **is** a battery that ... The electrodes in an XYZ telephone battery **are made** of a composite of gold and silver, coated with a layer of platinum. The gold and silver **provide** structural support, while the platinum **provides** resilience.

PRESENT PERFECT: how the problem has been approached from the past until the present day. In the examples, the exact time when the actions were carried out is NOT given.

> Computational techniques **have been extensively applied** to the study of the lifetime of XYZ batteries, in particular with regard to the number of times a battery is charged. However, little research to date **has focused** on the length of each individual recharge.

PAST SIMPLE: What specific authors have done, but in this case the year of publication of the journal is given.

> Celerata et al (2020) **extended** this idea by testing whether drivers of electric automobiles **respected** the highway code more than those with petrol-driven automobiles.

PAST SIMPLE: What the author (i.e. you) did and what your aim was.

> In our research **we investigated** whether ...

> **Our aim was** to reveal whether ...

PRESENT SIMPLE: at the end of the Introduction to explain the importance of your work, to introduce your results, and outline the structure of your paper.

> We **believe** that this is the first time that electrodes *have been investigated* from the point of view of ...

> The results of the model **show** that ...

> Section 2 **reviews** the literature. The methodology **is introduced** in Section 3. ...

2.6 What tenses are typically used in an Introduction and in the Review of the Literature? (cont.)

Note the use of the PRESENT PERFECT (*have been investigated*) in the first sentence. It is the equivalent of saying: *Electrodes have never been investigated from the ...* This construction is found after *This is the first time that ...* (i.e. it has never happened before).

1) Find an Introduction on your topic of research written by a native English-speaking author. Underline all the verbs. For each verb: i) identify the tense; ii) analyze if it matches the guidelines given above. For those tenses that do not match the guidelines, decide if there is a logical reason.

2) Check the tenses you used in the final exercise of 2.5.

2.7 Should I use a personal or impersonal style?

Most papers contain a mixture of a personal style (generally using active forms, and *we*) and an impersonal style (using the passive).

PASSIVE WHEN WE ARE NOT NECESSARILY INTERESTED IN WHEN SOMETHING WAS DONE OR BY WHO

> Computational techniques **have been extensively used** to study of the lifetime of XYZ batteries, in particular with regard to the number of times a battery **is charged**.

At this point in the paper, we are not necessarily interested in exactly when or who developed the 'computational techniques'.

ACTIVE WHEN REFERRING TO SPECIFIC AUTHORS

> Kidz et al. (2019) **found** that ...

> Celerata et al (2020) **extended** this idea by testing whether ...

The active form is used. It is clear to the reader who performed the action because the name of the author of the study is given.

PERSONAL PRONOUNS AND ACTIVE FORM TO ALERT READER THAT YOU ARE NOW TALKING ABOUT WHAT YOU DID IN YOUR RESEARCH

> In our research **we investigated** whether ...

> **Our aim was** to reveal whether ...

The active form is used with first person pronouns. The use of *we* and *our* makes it clear to the reader that the authors of the current paper made the investigation. Note the use of the simple past when talking about your aims – you cannot use the present perfect in such cases.

The use of a personal form (*we, our*) differentiates your work from other people's work. If you write

> <u>An investigation was carried out</u> to understand whether...

> <u>The</u> aim was to reveal whether ...

the reader may not be sure if YOU carried out the investigation or someone else, and whether this was YOUR aim or someone else's aim.

2.7 Should I use a personal or impersonal style? (cont.)

1) Compare the way you do something with how a family member, friend, or fellow student does the same thing. Make sure the differentiation is absolutely clear. Choose a few of the following. The way you:

> dress, drive, organize your time, react to criticism, resolve problems, socialize, study, take notes during a lecture

For example:

> *I tend to drive slowly, whereas Michela drives very fast.*

2) Rewrite what you wrote for exercise 1, but imagining you are writing a research paper. Instead of using the first person singular (*I*) use the first person plural (*we*), and instead of referring to your friend / family member / fellow student as *my friend* or *he / she*, use their surname + a date of publication. Generally speaking, use the past tense for the other person, and the present tense for yourself. But use other tenses if you feel they are appropriate.

For example:

> *Ferrari [2023] stated that the best approach to driving was to go at the maximum speed... On the other hand, our approach consists in driving slowly...*

Exercises

English for Academic Research: Writing Exercises

Active vs passive: Chapter 10

Tenses: Chapter 20

Chapter 3
Introduction: Part 2

3.1 Model 2: Introduction starting with how the state of the art justifies the aim of your research

If you are science student do NOT do this exercise, instead do the exercises in 2.5.

This subsection and 3.2 show examples of Introductions from the humanities and social sciences. Read both model 2 and 3. Then check with your chosen journal to see which model is most similar to the way Introductions are written in the journal.

Like all the extracts in this book, the research they describe is TOTALLY fictitious.

Note how in each paragraph the author introduces the work of other authors and then immediately compares it with her own work.

In 1726, Jonathan Swift was the first author to investigate the concept of 'endedness', i.e. what can be learned from whether a person breaks their egg at the big end (big-endians) or small end (small-endians). The concept of endedness was then forgotten for nearly three centuries.

Three main studies have recently approached the issue of endedness in terms of whether big-endians (BEs) or small-endians (SEs) are more likely to act selfishly, i.e. to think of their own interests and needs before those of others. Bama et al. (2022) found that children of BE parents in the USA were less inclined to collaborate with their schoolmates, both in homework and sports activities, than children whose parents were SEs. Bama's study was replicated in two studies carried out in Europe (Itsekäs et al, 2024; Sebičen, 2025) which reported very similar results. *In our study,* which was carried out in three countries in Asia, *we aimed* to challenge this position by showing that children behave similarly, irrespectively of how they were brought up to break their eggs.

© The Author(s), under exclusive license to Springer Nature
Switzerland AG 2022
A. Wallwork, *Writing an Academic Paper in English*, English for Academic
Research, https://doi.org/10.1007/978-3-030-95615-8_3

3.1 Model 2: Introduction starting with how the state of the art justifies the aim of your research (cont.)

Celerata et al (2026) extended the relationship between endedness and selfishness by testing whether drivers of cars who were BEs respected the highway code less than their SE counterparts. They found that BEs were more likely to incur speeding fines, parking tickets and to go through traffic lights on red. However, Celerata's results have been contested by several researchers (Ca di Lac et al., 2026), and have not been confirmed by similar studies conducted in the UK (Rolls & Royce, 2027), Sweden (Volvo et al, 2028) and South Korea (Kia et al, 2030). In fact, *in our research we investigated* whether driving habits may thus be due not primarily to egg-breaking habits, but also to age and gender.

Thus only some studies have indicated that selfishness may be predictable based on endedness. *In our study, we* set up a controlled environment with two samples of 100 people each, one made up of BEs and the others Ses. *Our aim* was to reveal whether someone's egg-breaking habits are more or less likely to make them act selfishly. To achieve this aim we analysed x, y, and z.

Follow the model given above and examples given points 1–4 in subsection 2.4, and write one paragraph introducing your topic. You can invent any information you want. Use a scientific style of writing.

3.2 Model 3: Introduction with chronology of previous papers. Author's own paper introduced at the end.

Below is a very similar Introduction to the one given in Model 2. This time the author lists all the previous work in chronological order before introducing her own work. This style tends to be used in humanistic papers. As you read, think about which style is more effective: Model 2 or Model 3.

PARA 1 Selfishness has been defined as a lack of consideration for other people. In its most extreme form it is known as egomania. Selfishness differs from narcissism, which manifests itself in obsessive self-love and is a psychological disorder, whereas selfishness is associated with inconsiderate behavior.

PARA 2 Selfishness has only recently been studied in terms of endedness, i.e. what can be learned from whether a person breaks their egg at the big end (big-endians - BEs) or small end (small-endians- SEs). Bama et al. (2022) found that children of BE parents in the USA were less inclined to collaborate with their schoolmates both in homework and sports activities, than children whose parents were SEs. Bama's study was replicated in two studies carried out in Europe (Itsekäs et al, 2024; Sebičen, 2025), which produced very similar results. These studies suggested that there is a direct relationship between endedness and selfishness.

PARA 3 Celerata et al (2026) extended the relationship between endedness and selfishness by testing whether drivers of cars who were BEs respected the highway code less than their SE counterparts. They found that BEs were more likely to incur speeding fines, parking tickets and to go through traffic lights on red. However, Celerata's results have been contested by several researchers (Ca di Lac et al., 2026), and have not been confirmed by similar studies conducted in the UK (Rolls & Royce, 2027), Sweden (Volvo et al, 2028) and South Korea (Kia et al, 2030).. Driving habits may thus be due not primarily to egg-breaking habits, but also to age and gender (Volvo et al, 2021) and how extrovert they are (Loukatmi, 2022).

PARA 4 Thus only some studies have indicated that selfishness may be predictable based on endedness. Later experiments have shown that selfish behaviors manifest themselves much more clearly during crisis situations, both economic (Morgan, 2025) and virus-related (Vid, 2019).

Blah blah blah for several paragraphs

PARA 5 In our study, our aim was to reveal whether someone's egg-breaking habits are more or less likely to make them act selfishly. To achieve this aim we analysed x, y, and z.

3.2 Model 3: Introduction with chronology of previous papers. Author's own paper introduced at the end. (cont.)

Model 3 is structured as follows:

PARAGRAPH 1: The first sentence introduces the general topic (selfishness) through a definition. Selfishness is then distinguished from a related behavior, narcissism.

PARAGRAPH 2: The main topic of the paper is introduced (endedness and how this effects selfish behaviors) with a key paper in the field (Bama). Papers that confirm Bama's findings are then listed. The implications of these studies are summarized at the end of the paragraph.

PARAGRAPH 3: The first sentence moves on to the next (in chronological terms) major study in the field of endedness and selfishness. This time the main example paper (Celerata) is contrasted with other papers that did not confirm Celerata's findings. Again, some general conclusions are summarized.

PARAGRAPH 4: Summarizes the findings of Paragraphs 2 and 3 in order to introduce some more recent findings.

FINAL PARAGRAPH: Author introduces his/her own work.

The above structure is very typical of Introductions written in fields of the humanities, social sciences and economics / business studies. Personally, I think this structure works well in a textbook where you are explaining the background to your research to a more general audience. However, if you are writing in a specific journal, your readers are possibly less interested in the history of your research area (which they may already be familiar with), and more interested in how these studies directly compare with yours.

Model 2 is a better way of introducing the context of your work than Model 3. Model 2 makes constant comparisons so the reader understands continuously how the author's work fits in with previous work. In Model 3, the reader has to wait until the end of the Introduction before understanding how this new paper builds on previous papers.

3.2 Model 3: Introduction with chronology of previous papers. Author's own paper introduced at the end. (cont.)

I suggest you try using the structure in Model 2, using the following steps. Note each step may require more than one paragraph.

STEP 1: introduce topic by citing the first main studies in your field. End this section by saying your aim differs from these studies

STEP 2: quickly review other studies in your field that continued the work of the authors. Highlight their good points and also their drawbacks. Say how your research aims to overcome these drawbacks.

STEP 3: make a mini summary of the progress that has been made so far in your field and underline again how your work is designed to rectify the drawbacks and/or advance on current knowledge.

Exercises

English for Academic Research: Writing Exercises Defining, comparing, evaluating and highlighting: Chapter 8

3.4 Typical mistakes made in Introductions

The main mistakes made in Introductions are:

- they are too long

- there is too much background info

- the papers reviewed are simply listed chronologically, the authors do not discuss the papers they mention in relation to their own paper

- it is <u>not</u> clear when the author is talking about their own work or is talking about what other researchers have done

Another key problem is that there is a lot of redundancy, i.e. ten words are used where one or two would be enough. This often happens when the author is describing what other authors have done. It is a problem because this kind of writing, with many superfluous (unnecessary) words, makes it tedious for the reader, who may then decide to stop reading.

Compare these pairs of sentences. The first sentence contains redundancy, the second sentence is more concise. What techniques are used to make the sentences more concise?

1. Redundancy *is known to be* characteristic of poor readability [Gharbij et al, 2024].

   Redundancy *is* a characteristic of poor readability [Gharbij et al, 2024].

2. *In the literature* redundancy *has also been reported* in languages other than English [Prolix et al, 2020].

   Redundancy *is* not exclusive to English [Prolix et al, 2020].

3. The use of long sentences *has been ascertained* in *various regions of* Europe during the Roman period [Caesar, 2019].

   Long sentences *were used* during the Roman period in Europe [Caesar, 2019].

4. *The concept of* redundancy *has been suggested as playing* a role in the construction of long sentences [Stodge, 2025].

   Redundancy *may play* a role in the construction of long sentences [Stodge, 2025].

5. *Several authors* [Nadmierność, 2019; Kalabisan, 2020; Liiallisuus, 2022] *have proposed* that in scientific writing the occurrence of redundancy *is* correlated to …

   In scientific writing the occurrence of redundancy *may* be correlated to … [Nadmierność, 2019; Kalabisan, 2020; Liiallisuus, 2022].

3.4 Typical mistakes made in Introductions (cont.)

1) The present tense (*is*) already indicates that something exists or is known. So, it is unnecessary to use *known to be*.

2) When you put a reference (e.g. *Prolix et al, 2020*) it is clear that you are talking about *the literature*. Also, given that this sentence would appear in the review of the literature, the reader automatically understands that you are talking about the literature. Try to avoid unnecessary uses of verbs such as *report, highlight, found, show, demonstrate, suggest, propose* etc.

3) Avoid vague phrases (*various regions of* Europe). Instead either state the precise regions (e.g. Italy, Turkey) or simply cut the phrase.

4) Avoid abstract words that add no value (*the concept of*). Consider using modal verbs (*can, may, should* etc) to replace long expressions (*has been suggested as playing*).

5) Same issues as in 2, 3 and 4.

Find an Introduction from an online paper in your field. Copy and paste the texts into a Word file. Then delete any words and phrases that you don't think are important.

Finally, compare your version with the original version:

- Have you removed any key concepts?

- Do the key concepts now stand out so that they are clearer for your recipient?

- Is your version quicker and simpler to read?

Now analyse two or three emails you have written, either in English or your own language. Find ways to make them shorter and/or more precise.

3.5 Why are reducing the length of an article and avoiding redundancy so important?

Many unnecessarily long papers are published, as well as papers full of redundancy. So you may think that length and redundancy are not important.

In fact, most referees, reviewers and editors make no comments about papers that are unnecessarily long. This is because their main job is to check the scientific content, they are not English teachers! Often they simply don't have time to make comments about the style of the English, though they will normally mention grammatical mistakes, typos, and unclear phrases.

But being published is NOT the most important thing (see 1.2). Being published AND READ is what is important.

Which would you prefer to read a paper that is 40 pages long, or one that is 20 pages long and contains exactly the same information but expressed more succinctly?

The fact is most readers don't have time to read every word, every sentence, every paragraph or even every section. They want information quickly. They want to see the key words and have the key results highlighted for them.

So if you want to be successful as an academic, remember that you need to make it pleasurable to read your paper. If you fill your paper with redundant words and phrases, your readers may think it is not worth their effort and time to read it.

English for Writing Research Papers

    Chapter 5 Being Concise and Reducing Redundancy

English for Academic Research: Writing Exercises.

    5.26 reducing the length of an introduction

    5.27 reducing the length of the outline of the structure

    5.28–5.29 reducing the length of the review of the literature

100 Typical Mistakes Chapter 2

3.6 Do's and Don'ts of writing the Introduction

DON'T forget that language editors often find that the worst parts of a paper written by a non-native English speaker are the Introduction and the Discussion.

DON'T make general statements that are already widely known.

DO give the reader the tools for understanding the meaning and motivation of your experiments.

DO make it clear what problem you are addressing and why you chose your particular methodology.

DO tell your readers how you plan to develop your topic and what the structure of your paper is.

DON'T start thinking about the Introduction after you have written the other parts of the paper. Instead, write notes for your Introduction while you are doing your research, i.e. BEFORE you have begun even thinking about writing a paper. During your research, whenever you read another paper on your topic, note down the similarities and differences between what YOU are doing (or plan to do) and what THEY (the authors of the other papers) have done. Think about how the research YOU are carrying out is an extension and improvement on what THEY have done. If you make these notes BEFORE you write the paper, then you will find the Introduction much easier to write. These notes comparing YOUR work with THEIR work will also help you when you write the Discussion.

3.7 Useful phrases

Note: Many of the typical phrases you will need in an Introduction are the same as those needed for an Abstract (see 10.7).

1 KEY TERMINOLOGY IN YOUR FIELD

X is defined by Peng [2020] to refer to / to mean …

The term 'X' is generally understood to mean / has come to be used to refer to / has been applied to …

Several authors have attempted to define X, but as yet / currently / at the time of writing *there is still no accepted definition.*

2 PANORAMA OF PAST-TO-PRESENT LITERATURE

Many / Few *studies have been published on* … [Ref]

In the literature there are many / several / a surprising number of / few *examples of* …

Various approaches have been proposed / put forward / suggested / hypothesized *to solve this issue [Ref].*

X has been identified / indicated *as being* … [Ref]

X has been shown / demonstrated / proved / found *to be* … *[Ref]*

Xs have been receiving / gaining *much attention due to* …

3 REVIEWING THE LITERATURE

In 2023, Doyle was among / one of *the first to* …

Experiments on X were conducted / carried out / performed *on X in 2019 by a group of researchers from* …

In a major advance in 2024, Yin et al surveyed / interviewed …

In [67] the authors investigated / studied / analyzed …

Since 2021 / In the last few years, *much more information on X has become available* …

Several studies, for example / instance *[1], [2], and [6],* have been carried out / conducted / performed *on X.*

More recent evidence [Southern, 2026] shows / suggests / highlights / reveals /

A recent review of the literature on this topic / subject / matter / area *highlights that* …

3.7   Useful phrases (cont.)

4 WHAT SPECIFIC AUTHORS OF HAVE STATED

In her analysis / review / overview / critique *of X, Bertram [2] questions the need for ...*

In his introduction to / seminal article on / investigation into *X, Schneider [3] shows that ...*

She questions / wonders / considers / investigates *whether [or not] X can ...*

They make / draw *a distinction between ...*

He claims / argues / maintains / suggests / points out / underlines *that ...*

Her theory / solution / proposal / method / approach *is based on ...*

She concludes / comes to the conclusion / reaches the conclusion *that ...*

5 LIMITATIONS OF PREVIOUS STUDIES

The main limitation / downside / disadvantage / pitfall / shortfall *of X is ...*

Research has tended to focus on X rather than Y. An additional problem is that / Moreover *X is ...*

One of the major drawbacks to adopting / using / exploiting *this system is ...*

Unfortunately, it does not / fails to / neglects to *explain why ...*

Peng [31] claimed / contended *that X is ... but she failed to provide adequate proof of this finding.*

The main weakness in their study is that they make no attempt to ... / offer no explanation for ... / they overlook ...

6 STRUCTURE OF THE PAPER

This paper is organized as follows / divided into five sections.

The first section / Section 1 *gives a brief overview of ...*

The second section examines / analyses ...

In the third section a case study is presented / analyzed ...

A new methodology is described / outlined *in the fourth section ...*

Some / Our *conclusions are drawn in the final section.*

3.8   Exercises

1) Analyse the verbs in bold. Correct the ones that you think are in the wrong tense.

1. For the last few years researchers **are studying** the problem of x.

2. Good writing **has been defined** as telling the reader only what he/she needs to know.

3. We believe that this is the first time that this problem **is studied**.

4. Our aim **has been** to study how X reacts to Y.

5. Smith et al. (2019) **found** that X is equal to Y.

6. Three main studies (Jones, 2020; Yin, 2021; Re, 2023) **have approached** the issue of X in terms of Y.

7. Section 2 **reviews** the literature. The methodology **is introduced** in Section 3. ...

2) Complete the sentences below. X refers to your topic of research, an element of your topic, an approach, a methodology, a piece of equipment etc.

1. In the literature, X usually refers to ___

2. In the literature there are many examples of ___

3. What is known about X is largely based on ___

4. On the other hand, few studies have been published on ___

5. Little is known about ___

6. In recent years there has been considerable interest in ___

7. The first studies on X found that ___

8. In the last few years ___

9. The main limitation of X is ___

10. There is still considerable uncertainty with regard to ___

3) Write a short paragraph for each heading below. You can use the useful phrases (3.6) to help you.

1. The key terminology used in your field.

2. A general panorama of the literature in your field from past to present.

3. A description of a group of papers in your field that cover similar ground to you.

4. The limitations of the studies you mentioned in Point 3.

3.8   Exercises (cont.)

5. How your work resolves the limitations of previous studies.

6. The structure of your paper.

Exercise 1 1) *have been studying* (this action began in the past and is continuing into the present. So there is a mix of past and present, and in this case the present perfect continuous is correct); 2) correct; 3) *has been studied* (this implies it has never been studied before - the present perfect is required); 4) *was* (your aim is something that you established at the beginning of your research; it would also be possible to say *our aim is*, but the past is the most suitable. The present perfect is NOT possible in such cases); 5–7) correct. Do not use *will* when you are outlining the structure of your paper (7) – in a scientific paper, just use *will* to refer to a real future event.

English for Academic Research: Writing Exercises

> How to be concise: 5.26–5.29

> Paraphrasing and avoiding plagiarism: Chapter 7

> Making generalizations: 8.4

> Structure: 10.2–10.5

English for Academic Research: Vocabulary Exercises

> Typical phrases: 8.1–8.7

100 Typical Mistakes

> Chapter 2

English for Writing Research Papers

> Writing the Introduction: Chapter 14

> Writing the Review of the Literature: Chapter 15

Chapter 4
Methods

4.1 What is a Methods section?

This section of a paper has several different names including: 'Methods', 'Methods and Materials', 'Experimental', 'Method Description and Validation'. In this chapter, I will always refer to it as Methods. It may also be divided up into several parts, each with its own heading.

In most journals the Methods section follows the Literature Review, in others it follows the Conclusions.

Imagine that some friends have asked you to send them the recipe for your favorite dish.

You would need to tell them:

- the ingredients
- the kitchen tools and equipment they need
- the various steps involved – in chronological order
- the exact amounts of each ingredient
- the name of the equipment, the settings on the equipment, and how the equipment was used
- how the dish should look when it is ready
- anything that should accompany the dish (other food, other tools needed)

Essentially you need to tell them EVERYTHING they need to know in order to replicate your recipe in their own kitchen.

And this is what a Methods section aims to do: it should enable other researchers to replicate in their laboratory what you did in your laboratory.

© The Author(s), under exclusive license to Springer Nature Switzerland AG 2022
A. Wallwork, *Writing an Academic Paper in English*, English for Academic Research, https://doi.org/10.1007/978-3-030-95615-8_4

4.1 What is a Methods section? (cont.)

This activity requires you to work with a partner.

Choose one of the activities (a–j) below.

What steps do you take to?

a) choose where to go on holiday (e.g. get recommendations from friends, decide a budget, decide means of transport, go on Trip Advisor, identify location and accommodation, book tickets etc)

b) make a cup of coffee

c) clean your computer screen

d) edit and revise your own writing

e) get reliable news

f) keep yourself cool / warm during hot / cold periods

g) organize your files on your PC

h) prioritize what you are going to do during your day

i) protect your private data

j) stay awake during online university lectures

Describe the various steps in detail to your partner. When your have finished, you partner should then try to summarize the steps. When they have finished, discuss these questions:

- What steps, if any, did your partner forget? Why? Had you explained them clearly?

- Did you explain all the steps in chronological order or at least the most logical order?

- In your description, what were the most important steps? Did your partner realise that these were important steps? Had you highlighted how important they were?

Now your partner should tell you their method for the activity they have chosen from a–j.

4.1 What is a Methods section? (cont.)

Given that you are very familiar with your research method, you may leave out <u>key</u> information either thinking that it is implicit (and thus not worth mentioning) or simply because you forget. So, ensure that you cover every step required. However, you also need to be concise, so avoid any unnecessary detail.

4.2 Model 1: Medical, technical

Below is an extract from the Methods section to a fictitious medical paper. The language used and the structure are similar to most Methods sections in medical / scientific / technical papers.

PARA 1 An egg-breaking disorder (also known as *eggoism*) is defined as a medical condition where a person is confused as to which end of the egg they should break, which then has a detrimental impact on the way they interact with family members and the community.

PARA 2 We retrospectively analysed clinical and psychological features of 159 patients associated with egg-breaking disorders, presenting consecutively at the Department of Eggology, University of Atlantis between 2025 and 2028. The study was approved by the ethics committee and informed consent was obtained from all patients.

PARA 3 The data were taken from computerized medical records and the brain scans were taken from the database of a 3D imaging system (Yoke™). The egg-breaking history of the patients had been previously confirmed by medical reports provided by the patient's psychologist. Patients who had shown violent or psychotic behaviours during sessions with their psychologist were not included.

PARA 4 We analysed the brain scans of all the patients to locate the position of the neurons in the brain that were responsible for decisions regarding which end of the egg to break.

PARA 5 The gravity of the egg-breaking disorder was then measured according to the formula developed by Eghed et al (2026):

$$\left(D = \Delta L / Ebs \right)$$

where D represents disorder, ΔL is the location of the neurons, and E is the predominant egg breaking habit (b – big end, s – small end).

PARA 6 We statistically compared the levels of the disorder using an analysis of variance test (ANOVA). This test enabled us to establish the differing levels of the disorder in relation to ΔL.

4.2   Model 1: Medical, technical (cont.)

1. The text is divided into six paragraphs. What is the function of each paragraph?

2. What style does the author use: (a) impersonal (only passive), (b) personal (we + active), (c) a mix?

3. Only two tenses are used. Which ones: (a) simple past (*we tested*), (b) present perfect (*we have tested*), (c) past perfect (*we had tested*)

4. In the penultimate sentence (*This test enabled us to establish the differing levels*) is 'us' necessary? Could we simply say 'enabled/permitted / allowed to establish'?

1) The structure below is just one possible structure. I suggest you look at a journal in your field and analyse the structure of the Methods section in some of the papers.

   PARAGRAPH 1: definition, overview of topic. You may have mentioned this in the Introduction (and even in the Abstract). But you cannot be sure that the reader has read the Abstract and Introduction, they may start with the Methods.

   PARAGRAPH 2: sample (in this case medical patients)

   PARAGRAPH 3: source of data

   PARAGRAPH 4: procedure

   PARAGRAPH 5: measurements

   PARAGRAPH 6: validity of test

2) c

3) a, c. The past perfect is used to refer to information relating to things that had happened before the researcher's study began.

4) *us* is necessary. The construction is to *allow/enable/ permit* someone to do something. However often a simpler solution is possible e.g. *The test established / highlighted / revealed the differing levels.*

4.3   Methods Model 2: Engineering, chemistry, physics

Below is a very short extract from the Methods section to a paper that used sensors to measure the stress on a robotic arm when lifting a heavy load. The <u>underlined</u> words are mine.

A <u>3 mm</u> thick filter with a frame of 11 samples was applied to the signals in order to reduce the noise. <u>A total of 25</u> filters were used to test each brain scan. The effects of these filters are shown <u>in Fig. 2</u>.

Figure 2 highlights that the filter removes most of the noise, thereby revealing the behavior of the signal.

This type of filter eliminates the noise without altering the true signal peaks.

1. Unlike Model 1 which only uses past tenses, Model 2 uses the simple present (*is used*) and simple past (*was used*). Underline all the verbs and try to understand the logic of using the past rather than the present, and vice versa.

2. The word *figure* appears three times. The first time it is abbreviated (*Fig.* 2) but the other times the full word is used (*Figure 2*). Do you know why?

1) *was applied* – in this case the detection and application were carried out by the author during her experiments in the laboratory. This detection and application are totally finished actions.

is shown / highlights – the author is referring to her paper, NOT what she did in the lab. Figure 2 highlights something for the reader NOW.

eliminates – like *performs* this is a general attribute, i.e. not something that happened during the experiments.

2) *table* and *figure*: when associated with a number, require an initial capital T and F. There is no abbreviation for table. The abbreviation for *figure* is *Fig.* – with a period after the *g*. See 5.4. in *Grammar, Usage and Strategies*.

4.3   Methods Model 2: Engineering, chemistry, physics (cont.)

Model 2 contains several numbers, which I have <u>underlined</u>.

Most journals recommend using words for numbers from one to ten, and then digits. However this rule does not apply when the number precedes an abbreviation for a measurement (e.g. *3 mm*). There are no clear rules about whether to write 3 mm or 3mm. Using 3mm means that the two parts (i.e. the number and the abbreviation) will not become separated, for instance at the end of a line.

Note also that abbreviations for measurements do not have an *s* when they are plural (e.g. *3 mm*, not *3 mms*).

Don't begin a sentence with a number in digits, instead use A total of (e.g. *a total of 25 filters*). For details on the use of numbers see 5.3–5.6 in *Grammar, Usage and Strategies*.

4.4 Methods Model 3: Social / Political sciences

In the extract below, the language used and the structure are similar to most Methods sections in disciplines related to social and political sciences.

Note. The research is fictitious. However, Perry's scale and Cronbach's formula are real.

Data were collected between April and October 2026 primarily from semi-structured interviews carried out in 17 member countries of the European union. Interviewees were asked to complete a questionnaire (see Appendix 1). All measures (Table 1) were assessed using responses to a 5-point Likert scale ranging from 1 (total disagreement) to 5 (total agreement). The level of egoism (LeO) was measured as the mean of the standardized values of the following items: (a) 'I have no problem driving while using my phone'; (b) 'I often leave litter behind on a beach'; and (c) 'I happily play very loud music in the middle of the night'. The three-item scale for LeO was developed following Gung Ho et al. (2022).

On the other hand, self-sacrifice (SS) was measured as the mean of the following standardized items according to Perry's scale: (a) 'I believe in putting duty before self'; (b) 'I am prepared to make enormous sacrifices for the good of society'; and (c) 'Making a difference in society means more to me than personal achievements'.

Answers to the questions were then analysed using a varimax rotation. Scale reliability and variance-extracted measures showed encouraging results: Cronbach's alpha was satisfactory for egoism and lack of social commitment (0.70) and empathy / self-sacrifice (0.78).

1. The author only uses an impersonal form – every verb is in the passive. Why is it clear to the reader that all the actions (*were collected, were asked, was measured, was developed* etc) were carried out by the author?

2. What do these <u>underlined</u> words and phrases mean: <u>following</u> Gung Ho et al. ... <u>according to</u> Perry's scale

3. What does the apostrophe (') indicate in Perry's and Cronbach's?

4.4   Methods Model 3: Social / Political sciences (cont.)

1) This is the Methods section, and unless the author indicates otherwise, the reader can assume that the methods were followed by the author of this paper and not by another author. If you mention another author's methods then make sure you put their name, e.g. _We used an xyz. On the other hand, Pisteik et al [2025] used pqr._

2) They mean that the author of the present paper used a method (protocol, formula, etc) of another author.

3) The apostrophe indicates the genitive form (see 12.6. in _Grammar, Usage and Strategies_). Perry's scale is a scale established by a researcher named J.L.Perry who identified a 24-item multidimensional scale to measure public service motivation. The genitive form indicates that this scale belongs to (is due to, was invented by) Perry. Similarly, Lee Cronbach was an American educational psychologist who researched into psychological testing and measurement. Cronbach's alpha is a formula he invented to provide a measure of reliability.

Think about the examinations you have done at university. Use the structure below to summarize in a scientific/formal way the examination process.

1. aim of the examinations

2. organization of the exam process by your department (e.g. how often organized, where held, who eligible to partake)

3. method you used to prepare for the exams

4. structure of the exams (e.g. number of questions/parts, time allowed, 'equipment' permitted for use during the exam)

5. method used by examiners to assess your performance

Note: In exercise 5.3, you will have a chance to continue this exercise, i.e. by talking about the results (marks, scores) you got.

4.5 Style and tenses typically used in the Methods section

PASSIVE FORM / PAST SIMPLE

Your readers will know that it is your work, so you don't need to say *we did this, we did that*, instead you can say *this was done, that was done*. However, if you want you can use a mixture of passive and active.

Data **were collected** [PASSIVE] between April and October 2023. Interviewees **were asked** [PASSIVE] to complete a questionnaire. **We assessed** [ACTIVE] the measures using responses to a 5-point Likert scale.

PRESENT SIMPLE

1) What is already known: i) facts <u>not</u> found by you, but by others in the scientific community; ii) characteristics of a certain entity.

This type of filter **eliminates** the noise without altering the true signal peaks.

2) To refer to figures, tables, graphs etc.

Figure 2 **highlights** that the filter removes most of the noise, thereby revealing the behavior of the signal.

3) For habitual actions.

I happily **play** very loud music in the middle of the night.

Find a Methods section on your topic of research written by a native English speaking author. Underline all the verbs. For each verb: i) identify the tense; ii) analyse if it matches the guidelines given above. For those tenses that do not match the guidelines, decide if there is a logical reason.

4.6 Do's and Don'ts

DO write the Methods section before the other section. Researchers generally agree that the Methods is the easiest section to write because your methods are likely to be clear in your mind.

DO analyse two or three Methods section in the journal where you plan to publish your paper. Use them as a template.

DO make it clear to the reader why you chose a particular method and why you did NOT choose another method.

DON'T have too much information in the same sentence as it makes it hard for the reader to follow. At the same time, your Methods section is not simply a list of actions, try to show the logical connection between each action.

DON'T write too much – just the details necessary for your readers to replicate your work. This means that if you want your Methods to be easy to follow, you need to: (i) reduce the number of words; (ii) assume your readers have basic knowledge of the techniques used in your field, so delete any superfluous information; (iii) refer readers to previous work where the method or well-known parts of it are described; and (iv) use tables and figures to summarize information.

DO construct your sentences in a logical way, one step at a time. The following sentence below is not logical in its order: The plant, which was then sprayed with copper, had been treated with fertilizer in a greenhouse. It might be more logical to say that first it was treated with fertilizer and then with copper.

DON'T just say WHAT you did, but also the CONSEQUENCE of what you did. Example: We sprayed the plant with copper, <u>thus</u> protecting it from fungicides.

DO use bullet points if this will highlight a sequence of steps more clearly. But check whether your journal allows bullet points.

DO use headings if your Methods (or any other part of the paper) is long. Such headings could be, for example: sampling procedure, participants, materials, experimental setup, design, software used, procedure, testing the model.

4.6 Do's and Don'ts (cont.)

Find some Methods sections in a journal in your field. How are they constructed? Does each paragraph have a clear aim / topic?

If the author only uses one paragraph for the entire Methods, then note down the purpose of each sentence or group of sentences.

Finally, note if the language and structure of the Methods are similar to one of the three models outlined in 4.2–4.4. Also note any significant differences.

Finally adapt either one of the three models or one of the methods from the journal. Use it to describe a recent experiment that you carried out during your research.

4.7 Useful phrases

7 PURPOSE OF TESTING / METHODS USED

To see / determine / check / verify / determine *whether* …

In order to identify / understand / investigate / study / analyze *X* …

So that we could / would be able to *do X, we* …

In an attempt / effort *to do X, we* …

X was done / We did X *in order to* …

To enable / allow *us to do x, we* …

To enable / allow *x to be done, we* …

8 APPARATUS AND MATERIALS

The instrument used / utilized / adopted / employed *was* …

The apparatus consists of / is made up of / is composed of / is based on …

The device was designed / developed / set up *in order to* …

The system is equipped / is fully integrated / is fitted *with a* …

It is mounted on / connected to / attached to / fastened to / fixed to / surrounded by / covered with / integrated into / embedded onto / encased in / housed in / aligned with …

It is located in / situated in / positioned on ….

X was obtained from / supplied by *Big Company Inc.*

X was kindly provided / supplied *by Prof Big.*

9 SOFTWARE

We used commercially available software / a commercially available software package.

The data were obtained / collected *using SoftGather.*

X was carried out / performed / analyzed / calculated / determined *using SoftGather.*

Free software, downloaded from www.free.edu, was used / adopted *to* …

The set-up we used can be found / is reported / is detailed *in [Ref 2].*

We refined / altered / adapted / modified / revised *the method* used / reported / suggested / explained / proposed / put forward *by Knut [2024].*

We used a variation of Smith's procedure. In fact / Specifically, *in our procedure we* …

4.7   Useful phrases (cont.)

The procedure used is as described / explained / reported / proposed *by Sakamoto [2023].*

More details can be found / are given *in our previous paper [35].*

X was tailored / customized *for use with …*

Measurements were taken using purpose-built / custom-built / customized *equipment.*

The apparatus was adapted as in [Ref] / in accordance with [Ref] / as follows:

The following changes / modifications *were made:*

11 EQUATIONS, THEORIES AND THEOREMS

This problem can be outlined / phrased / posed *in terms of …*

The problem is ruled by / governed by / related to / correlated to …

This theorem asserts / states *that …*

The resulting integrals / solution to X *can be expressed as …*

… where T stands for / denotes / identifies / is an abbreviation for *time.*

By substituting / Substituting / Substitution *into …*

Combining / Integrating / Eliminating *… we have that: …*

Taking advantage of / Exploiting / Making use of *X, we …*

On combining this result with X, we deduce / conclude *that …*

Subtracting X from Y, we have that / obtain / get …

Equation 1 shows / reveals *that*

It is straightforward / easy / trivial *to verify that …*

For the sake of simplicity / reasons of space, *we*

12 REASONS FOR CHOOSING YOUR SPECIFIC METHOD, MODEL, EQUIPMENT, SAMPLE

The aim / purpose *of X is to do Y.* Consequently we / As a result we / Therefore we / We thus …

This method / model / system *was chosen because it is one of the most* practical / feasible / economic / rapid *ways to …*

We chose this particular apparatus because / on account of the fact that / due to / since …

4.7 Useful phrases (cont.)

We opted for / chose *a small sample size* because / due to / on the basis of …

By having / By exploiting / Through the use of *X, we were able to* …

Having an X enabled us to / allowed us to / meant that we could *do Y.*

13 PREPARATION OF SAMPLES, SOLUTIONS ETC

We used reliable / innovative / classic / traditional *techniques based on the recommendations of* …

Xs were prepared as described by / according to / following *Jude [2010]*.

Xs were prepared in accordance with / in compliance with / as required by ….

Y was prepared using the same / a similar *procedure as for X.*

All samples were carefully / thoroughly *checked for* …

14 SELECTION PROCEDURE FOR SAMPLES, SURVEYS ETC

The traditional / classical / normal / usual *approach to sample collection is to* …

The criteria / reasons *for selecting Xs were*:

The sample was selected / subdivided *on the basis of X and Y.*

The initial sample consisted of / was made up / was composed of …

Approximately / Just over / Slightly under a half / third / quarter *of the sample were* …

A total of 1234 Xs were recruited for this study / this survey / for interviews.

In all cases patients' / subjects' / participants' *consent was obtained.*

Interviews were performed / conducted / carried out *informally*

The interviewees were divided / split / broken down *into two groups* based on / on the basis *of* …

15 TIME FRAME OF TESTS (PAST TENSES)

Initial studies were made / performed / done / carried out / executed *using the conditions described above* over / for *a period of* …

X was collected / used / tested / characterized / assessed *during the* first / initial *step.*

Prior to / Before doing *X, we did Y.*

First we estimated / determined *the value of X*, then / subsequently *we* studied / analyzed / evaluated *Y.*

Once / As soon as / After X *had been done, we then did Y.*

4.7 Useful phrases (cont.)

The levels were thus / consequently / therefore *set at* …

After / Afterwards / Following this, *X was subjected to Y.*

The resulting / remaining *Xs were then* …

The experiment was then repeated / replicated *under conditions in which* …

Finally, independent / separate / further / additional *tests were performed on the* …

16 TIME FRAME IN A GENERAL PROCESS (PRESENT TENSES)

In the first step / During the first phase / In the initial stage *of the process* …

Once / As soon as / After *X has been done, we can then do Y.*

At this point / Now *X can be* …

After / When / As soon as *these steps have been carried out, X* …

When / As soon as *X is ready, the final adjustments can be made.*

17 BENEFITS OF YOUR METHOD, EQUIPMENT ETC

This solution improves on / enhances / furthers / advances *previous methods by* …

This method represents a viable / valuable / useful / groundbreaking / innovative *alternative to* …

This equipment has the ability / capacity / potential *to outperform all previous Xs.*

This apparatus has several / many *interesting* features / characteristics.

Our method has many interesting / attractive / beneficial / useful / practical / effective / valuable *applications.*

We believe this solution will aid / assist *researchers to* …

4.8 Exercises

1) Choose a paper from your field of study. Look at the Methods section. Which of the following questions are answered and how are they answered? Complete the sentences.

1. What / Who did they study?

   They studied ___

   They wanted to ___

2. Where did they carry out this study and what characteristics did this location have?

   The study was ___

3. How did they design their experiment / sampling / model / protocol and what assumptions did they make?

   They designed their ____

4. What variables / parameters were they measuring and why?

   They measured ___

5. How did they handle / treat their materials / subjects? What kind of care / precautions were taken?

   The x was ___

   The following precautions ____

6. What equipment did they use (plus modifications) and where did this equipment come from (vendor source)?

   A _____ was used which was supplied by _____

7. How did they analyze the data? Statistical procedures? Mathematical equations? Software?

   In order to analyse the data, they _____

8. What data did they decide was significant and why?

   Data regarding ____ was considered significant because ____

9. What references to the literature did they give to save space by not having to describe something in detail?

   They did ____ in accordance with ____ (____).

10. What difficulties did they encounter?

    Problems regarding ____ arose due to ____

4.9 Exercises (cont.)

2) Write a short paragraph for those headings below that are relevant to your research. You can use the Useful Phrases (4.7) to help you.

1. The aims of your tests and methodology.

2. What equipment you used, why you used it, and how it is similar and different from the equipment used by others. Detail any modifications you made.

3. What software you used and for what purpose.

4. Explain the purpose and meaning of any formulas you used.

5. Detail the steps (in chronological order) that you made in order to develop, set up and implement your method / model / protocol etc.

6. Describe the benefits of the methodology / protocol / model etc that you used.

English for Academic Research: Writing Exercises

> Being concise: 5.30

> Describing processes, causes, effects: 4.13–4.15

> Writing definitions: 8.1–8.3

> Highlighting why your method is important: 8.7

> Comparing your methodology with other authors' methodologies: 8.11

> Reducing the length of the Methods section: 5.3

> Replacing *we* with the passive form: 7.6

> Structure: 10.6

English for Academic Research: Grammar Exercises

> Tenses: 21.2–21.4

English for Academic Research: Vocabulary Exercises

> Useful phrases: 8.7, 8.8

> Construction with *allow / enable / permit: 5.3*

100 Typical Mistakes

> 3.16–3.19

English for Writing Research Papers

> Writing the Methods: Chapter 16

Chapter 5
Results

5.1 What is the purpose of a Results section?

1) If you are interested in sports, do you look at ALL the results of EVERY match played, or just those of your favorite team and its rivals? Are you interested in unexpected results, for example when a team low in the division beats a team much higher up, or when one team gets an incredible score?

2) If there has been a political election, are you interested above all in the overall results, i.e. which party won or do you want to know everything about all the results? When you begin looking more in detail, do you look at the results of every part of your country, or do you tend to focus on the results in your areas and any surprise results (i.e. not predicted in the polls) in other parts of the country?

The Results section of a paper is something similar to the two examples given above. The reader is not interested in absolutely everything you found. Your job is to present the most relevant results: both those which confirm what you were expecting, and equally importantly those that contradict what you were expecting.

After a weekend's sports or after an election, newspapers tend to provide tables (e.g. of football results in the various divisions) and maps of election results. Often the election results are compared in charts with previous election results to show the progress (or lack of progress) of the various parties. Similarly in a Results section, you should exploit figures, tables, charts and maps as much as possible, and minimize the amount of text you use. Often readers just look at the tables, without actually reading the text in depth.

Not all journals require a separate Results section. Sometimes the results are integrated into the Discussion, under the section title Results and Discussion. If you have a separate Results section, then the standard procedure is to present them with little or no interpretation or discussion. This means that the Results is generally the shortest section in a paper.

© The Author(s), under exclusive license to Springer Nature
Switzerland AG 2022
A. Wallwork, *Writing an Academic Paper in English*, English for Academic
Research, https://doi.org/10.1007/978-3-030-95615-8_5

5.1   What is the purpose of a Results section? (cont.)

From an English point of view, the key skill is in reporting your results simply and clearly. If the referees of your paper cannot understand your results, then your contribution to the current knowledge base will be lost.

Decide which of the following you could illustrate with a figure, graph, table, chart or map. Then choose two, create your figures (graphs etc) and then describe the key results in a short text.

- the last election in your country / town

- your fitness program

- your favorite sport's team's performance last season

- a medical test you did recently (e.g. a blood test)

- an experiment you carried out

- your country's foreign policy last century

- your country's reaction to the last virus outbreak

- a diet that you tried

- your food expenditure over the last month divided up by weeks

5.2   Results Model 1: Medical, technical

Below is an extract from the Results section. The language used and the structure are similar to most Results sections in medical / scientific / technical papers.

We compared selfish behaviors in three key geographical areas: the USA, the EU, and four countries in Asia (China, Vietnam, Singapore and Taiwan). Using Eghed's alpha test, a positive correlation was observed between several selfish behaviors and endedness, i.e. whether someone breaks their egg at the big end (BE) or small end (SE).

The values from the Asian countries were surprisingly similar (see Supplementary Table 1), thus we decided to take median values rather than show each country separately. For Asia, we had no data on whether the subjects were BEs or SEs, and we were unable to establish their attitude towards queue jumping. The results for the EU and USA also show median values from the 27 and 50 states, respectively (see Supplementary Tables 2 and 3).

Our results showing the median values are summarized in Table 2. The table shows the percentages of people adopting a representative selection (5/10) of the antisocial behaviors investigated in our study. The full results for all 10 behaviors are given in Table S2 in the supplementary material.

ANTISOCIAL BEHAVIORS	US B	US S	EU B	EU S	ASIA FOUR
1. Double parking	78	74	80	75	10
2. Breaking speed limit	40	30	45	54	30
3. Dropping litter	70	40	76	35	8
4. Playing loud music late at night	40	38	32	34	10
5. Queue jumping	80	60	30	22	NA

Table 1 Comparison of propensity to commit selfish behaviours by big-enders and small-enders in the US (US B, US S); by big-enders and small-enders in the European Union (EU B, EU S), and all citizens in four Asian countries (Asia Four) irrespective of egg-breaking propensity. NA: data not available

5.2 Results Model 1: Medical, technical (cont.)

The results in Table 2 highlight that selfish behaviours in the US and EU do not differ substantially, with BEs showing more propensity to selfishness that SEs. There is one notable exception: i) BEs and SEs in the US are much more likely to jump a queue than citizens in Europe.

However, clearly the most significant result is the overall lack of selfish behaviors demonstrated by Asian citizens, with the exception of breaking the speed limit.

Analyse the example text and decide whether the following are true (T) or false (F). The author:

1. Begins with a one-line sentence summarizing what the authors did in their research.

2. Explains the use of abbreviations and terminology.

3. Uses lots of adjectives to underline the importance of their results.

4. Explains each result in detail.

5. Does not repeat in the text ALL the information that is shown in the table.

6. Mentions only key and unexpected results.

7. Uses a legend to explain the content of the table.

8. Uses long sentences and long paragraphs.

9. Refers readers to supplementary information that gives additional information that is not essential to understanding the main text.

1 T, 2 T, 3 F, 4 F, 5 T, 6 T, 7 T, 8 F, 9 T

5.3   Results: Model 2

/

Below is a shortened version of a Results section. In the experiments the authors made video recordings of people queueing outside cinemas.

Match the paragraphs (1–8) with their functions (a–h).

   a) brief comparison of results with the literature ___

   b) equipment / software used to evaluate data ___

   c) equipment / software used to evaluate data compared to the literature ___

   d) methodology recalled ___

   e) quick summary of meaning of results ___(Note: The full meaning will be in the Discussion)

   f) quick summary of purpose of research ___

   g) reference to figure / table to introduce and comment on first set of key results ___

   h) reference to figure / table to introduce and comment on second set of key results ___

PARA 1 Our aim was to note i) the percentage of people who jumped the queue (queue jumping behavior); ii) whether the length of the queue influenced the number of people who jumped the queue; iii) whether the genre of movie impacted on the likelihood of someone jumping the queue.

PARA 2 We used a mixture of CCTV footage plus videos posted on Instagram by people in the queue. The reason for this choice was to avoid privacy issues and to avoid having to ask people in the queue for permission to record them.

PARA 3 Figure 3 shows the relationship between the length of the queue and the episodes of queue jumping. The data highlight that in queues that contain ten or more people there is no difference in the probability that at least 1% of people will jump the queue on arrival. This number rises to 10% when it becomes evident to the queue jumper that they could save at least ten minutes by moving to the front of the queue.

PARA 4 Table 1 reports the association between genre of movie and the propensity to jump the queue. As can be seen, big-enders (BEs) queuing to see horror movies or movies with a high percentage of violence, are 30 times more likely to jump the queue than those small-enders (SEs) waiting to watch a romantic comedy.

5.3   Results: Model 2 (cont.)

PARA 5 The data on queue length in relation to queue jumping were analysed using Q-Master v. 12.1 (Q-Master Ltd, Manchester, UK). The association between someone's egg breaking habits, the genre of movie and propensity to jump the queue was measured using MonsterMovie v. 69.0 (Potworach, Warsaw). These two programs are open source and are frequently used in the literature for such analyses (Mooney, 2020; Czukay et al., 2021; Liebezeit, 2023).

PARA 6 Using the same data analysis techniques as the ones adopted in our work, Karoli et al. (2019) found that ... Suzuki et al. (2026) also found that ... which contradicts our findings given that ... In fact, we had some difficulty with ...

PARA 7 Our results are similar to Kwaku Baah (2018) who reported that ... However, a key difference is that ...

PARA 8 Our results would thus seem to indicate that being a big-ender rather than a small-ender, in conjunction with an interest in violence and a propensity to show aggressive behavior (even if non-violent), increases the chances of performing an antisocial selfish behavior such as a queue jumping.

a 7, b 5, c 6, d 2, e 8, f 1, g 3 h 4

1 f, 2 d, 3 g, 4 h, 5 b, 6 c, 7 a, 8 e

Some journals have just one section called 'Results and Discussion'. In such cases, paragraphs 6–8 would need expanding. However, if the Results and the Discussion are in two separate sections, then paragraphs 6–8 might not be necessary. Check with papers from your chosen journal to see which style is used.

The paragraphs in the text above about queue jumping are all short. In reality they would be longer as you would need to give more detail. However, like in the text, you need to start a new paragraph each time you talk about a different aspect of your results. If you just use one long paragraph readers will find it more difficult to understand i) what the results were, ii) why they are important; iii) how your results compare with other results.

Paragraph 6 in the queue jumping text has a phrase that begins *In fact, we had some difficulty with* ... It is important that you tell the reader about any difficulties you found or any unexpected results. If you have a separate Discussion section, this is usually where you inform your readers of such difficulties and then provide an explanation (see Chapter 6).

5.3   Results: Model 2 (cont.)

Look back at the exercise on your university examinations that you did in 4.5.

Think about all the exams you have done at university.

Choose some representative ones and not just the ones which you did well!

Remember any unexpected results (good and bad).

Now try to create a table of the results and a figure showing your progress.

When you have completed the table and figure write a text imagining that you were writing the Results section on a paper of your university successes and failures. Use the following structure:

1. quick summary of purpose and organization of examinations at your department

2. reference to figure / table to introduce and comment on first set of key results

3. reference to figure / table to introduce and comment on second set of key results

4. brief comparison of your results with those of fellow students

5. quick summary of the meaning of results (Note: The full meaning will be in the Discussion)

5.4 Writing about figures and tables

1. Do you like creating figures and tables? Do you use any particular applications to create them?

2. When you read an article or paper, do you tend to read the text first, or do you look at the tables and figures first?

3. If the figures and tables are clear, do you need to see a very detailed written explanation of what they contain?

4. In the Results section should you:

   a) detail all the results?

   b) highlight just the key results and any unexpected results?

   c) interpret and discuss the key and unexpected results?

Often, readers look at the tables and figures before reading the main text, as these contain a lot of information that can be absorbed very quickly (providing, of course, that the tables and figures are clear). If they are clear, then you don't need a detailed written explanation of what they mean. You just need to highlight the key points and any unexpected or surprising results. Generally, you <u>interpret</u> the results (i.e. say what you think they mean and what the implications are) in the Discussion section not in the Results section (so 4b is the correct answer).

This book is primarily about how to <u>write</u> in English, not about how to create tables and figures. However, there are many sites where you can learn these very important skills. Below are some documents that explain how to make your data meaningful to your audience (both academic and non-academic). Some of the documents are more than 15 years old, but they are nevertheless very useful.

https://ec.europa.eu/eurostat/documents/64157/4374310/33-UNECE-making-data-meaningful-Part2-EN.pdf/d5b954e2-b110-469b-a2b5-78aa7c12ab62

https://gss.civilservice.gov.uk/wp-content/uploads/2014/12/Effective-graphs-and-tables-in-official-statistics-version-1.pdf

https://www.intellspot.com/cool-ways-to-show-data/

You can also find many tutorials on YouTube, search for "presenting statistics".

5.4 Writing about figures and tables (cont.)

Find a paper in your field that has been frequently cited in other papers and is published in a journal with a high impact factor.

1. Do not read the paper, but just look at some of the tables and figures.

2. Choose one table or figure that you find easy to understand.

3. Decide what is the key information in the table or figure.

4. Report this key information, making comparisons where necessary. Avoid being too detailed, and do not interpret the data (this you will do in the Discussion – see 6.2).

5. Now compare what you have written with what the author wrote.

Repeat this exercise several times with several different articles. Note down:

- how many words on average the authors used to describe their tables

- what data in the table the author referred to, and what data the author did NOT refer to – try to understand why certain data were chosen but not others

When you write about your own tables and figures in the future, try to use a similar number of words as the authors of the texts you have analysed above, and try to focus only on reporting the same kind of data as the authors (as in the second bullet point above).

Using the same papers that you looked at in the previous exercise, analyse the structure of sentences used to describe the results. Which of the following constructions (a or b), does the author tend to use? Which do you think is more effective? Why?

1a) The xyz curve rises rapidly and peaks at 9.8. This peak indicates that ...

1b) The peak at 9.8 in the xyz curve indicates that ...

2a) The slow decrease in the curve of pqr is interesting. However, the rise in abc is also important.

2b) Interestingly, the curve of pqr decreases slowly, rather than rapidly. This is surprising because ... However, the rise in abc demonstrates that ...

5.4   Writing about figures and tables (cont.)

In both cases answer b is probably the best. The first sentence in 1a tells the reader nothing that they cannot understand by simply looking at the graph. 1b gives exactly the same information as 1a, but much more concisely, and the reader can understand immediately why the information is relevant.. 2a is very vague. Your readers want to know why something is *interesting* or *important*. On the other hand, 2b provides an explanation as to why this result is interesting and what the rise in abc means (you want to show your readers why it is important, without actually necessarily using the word *important*).

Moral of the story: In the Results (and in all the paper) be concise and precise. Being concise is very important in the Results section, as your key findings will stand out more if you avoid writing unnecessary words and phrases.

Note that the exercise above applies even more to the Discussion (see 6.2), where you interpret your results in more detail and compare them with the literature.

5.5   Tenses typically used in the Results

SIMPLE PAST to say:

* what your aim was

    Our aim **was** to understand the percentage of ...

* what you did in your research

    We **used** CCTV footage plus videos posted on Instagram.

    We **compared** selfish behaviors in three key geographical areas.

* what you found

    A positive correlation **was observed** ....

* your reasons for making certain choices

    The values from the Asian countries **were** surprisingly similar (see Supplementary Table 1), thus we **decided** to take median values rather than show each country separately.

    The reason for this choice **was** to avoid privacy issues.

* how data were analysed

    The data on queue length in relation to queue jumping **were analysed** using Q-Master v. 12.1

* what other authors found in their research

    Karoli et al. (2019) **found** that ...

SIMPLE PRESENT to say:

* where your results are shown

    Our results showing the median values **are summarized** in Table 2. The table **shows** the percentages of ...

* what your results mean

    The results in Table 2 **highlight** that ....

* how your results compare with others in the literature

    Our results **are** similar to Kwaku Baah (2018) who reported that ... However, a key difference **is** that ...

5.5 Tenses typically used in the Results (cont.)

WOULD to make tentative interpretations

Our results **would thus seem** to indicate that ...

Note the difference between *Our results indicate* (100% certainty) and *Our results would seem to indicate* (80–90% certainty). Using *would* protects you from readers and reviewers who may interpret your data differently. This practice is known as 'hedging' – see Chapter 10 in *English for Writing Research Papers* to learn more.

Find two Results sections on your topic of research written by native English speaking authors. Underline all the verbs. For each verb: i) identify the tense; ii) analyse if it matches the guidelines given above. For those tenses that do not match the guidelines, decide if there is a logical reason.

5.6   Do's and Don'ts of writing the Results

DO decide what results are representative. Organize them into a sequence that highlights the answers to the aims, hypotheses or questions that you mentioned in the Abstract / Introduction.

DO consider creating your tables and figures before you start writing the main text. Organize these tables and figures into the most logical order.

DON'T include all your findings. The problem is that readers may not be able to understand which findings are significant and which are not. So in the text just mention key findings. You can use tables in the main text and supplementary tables in an appendix to provide all the other findings.

DO give your readers the tools to understand the significance of your data.

DON'T repeat in the text everything that you have put in their figures and tables. This is very tedious for readers.

DON'T explain what commonly used statistical tests are or how they work. You can assume that readers know how to analyse statistics. However, you DO need to explain why one particular test was used rather than another.

DON'T omit findings simply because they don't support your hypotheses or other evidence.

DON'T forget to include any unexpected or contradictory findings.

5.7   Useful phrases

18 HOW YOU GOT YOUR RESULTS

To assess X / evaluate X / distinguish between X and Y, *Z was used.*

X analysis was used to test / predict / confirm *Y.*

Changes in X were identified / calculated / compared *using* …

The correlation / difference *between X and Y was tested.*

The first set of analyses investigated / examined / confirmed / highlighted *the impact of* …

19 TABLES AND FIGURES

Table 1 compares / lists / details / summarizes *the data on X.*

Table 2 proves / shows / demonstrates / illustrates / highlights *that X is* …

Figure 1 presents / reports / shows / details *the data on X.*

As shown / highlighted / illustrated / detailed / can be seen *in Fig. 1, the value of* …

The graph above / below / to the left / to the right *shows that* …

Figure 8 shows a clear trend / significant difference *in* …

20 WHAT YOU FOUND

As expected / predicted / hypothesized, *these tests* revealed / showed / highlighted *that* …

Strong / Some / No evidence *of X was found* …

Interestingly / Surprisingly / Unexpectedly / Counterintuively, *for high values of X, Y was found* …

On average / Generally speaking / Broadly speaking, *we found values for X of* …

The average / mean *score for X was* …

Further analysis / analyses / tests / examinations / replications *showed that* …

21 WHAT YOU DID NOT FIND

No significant difference / correlation *was* found / identified / revealed detected / observed / highlighted between ….

There were no significant differences between X and Y in terms of Z / with regard to Z / as far as Z is concerned.

5.7   Useful phrases (cont.)

The analysis did not show / reveal / identify / confirm *any significant differences between ...*

Overall / Taken as a whole / Generally speaking / With a few exceptions, *our results show X did not affect Y.*

22 RESULTS FROM QUESTIONNAIRES AND INTERVIEWS

Of the study population / initial sample / initial cohort, *90 subjects completed and returned the questionnaire.*

The response rate was 70% at / after / for the first *six months and ...*

The majority of respondents / those who responded *felt that ....*

Almost / Just under / Approximately *two-thirds of the participants (64%)* said / felt / commented *that ...*

In response to Question 1, most / nearly all / the majority *of those surveyed indicated that ...*

5.8 Exercises

1. Choose a paper from your field of study. Look at the Results section. Answer the questions below by writing:

a) yes b) not really c) no

1. Are you 100% clear which of the findings presented are the most important? ____

2. Was what the authors found what they were expecting? ___

3. In what format have they presented their data: (a) just text, b) text and figures / tables)? ___

4. If they used a lot of text, was all this text necessary? Could you have understood their findings without so much text? ___

5. Do their tables of results exclusively include data that prove their point? ___

6. Or have they also included data that did not match their expectations? ____

7. Did they mention any parts of their methodology (e.g. selection and sampling procedures) that could have affected their results? ____ If they didn't, is this a problem? ___

8. Does the paper have i) a separate Results section, or ii) is it part of a section called 'Results and Discussion'. ____

9. If the paper has a separate Results section, did the authors avoid making a lot of interpretations and drawing conclusions (NB interpretations and conclusions should be in the Discussion not the Results)?

10. After reading the Results, do you have a clear idea of what the authors found? ___ If so, would you be interested in seeing how they are interpreted in the Discussion? ___

When you write your own Results section, ask a colleague to review your section using the questions above. If your colleague answers *no* or *not really*, then you then to clarify your text.

2. Complete those sentences below that are most relevant to your particular research. You can use the Useful Phrases (5.7) to help you. Where necessary, change the words at the beginning of the sentences.

1. In one succinct sentence restate the aim of your research. This will help readers who start reading your paper by looking at the Results section, rather than the Abstract.

    Our aim was ___

5.8 Exercises (cont.)

2. Briefly remind your readers about your methodology and why you chose it.

    We used ____

    The reason for this choice was ___

3. Refer to a table or figure showing key results

    Figure 3 shows xyz and highlights ___

    Table 1 reports ___

4. Make a general statement about the results shown in the figure / table.

    The data shows / implies ___

5. Repeat Steps 3 and 4.

6. Mention what method you used to analyse your data.

    The data were analysed using a ___

    In line with Smith et al (2024), we analysed our data _____

7. Now talk specifically about some of the most significant results.

    A key finding revealed in our testing was ___

8. Compare one of your key findings with previous work. Simply comment on the differences without stating the implications (you will do this step in the Discussion).

    Jones et al (2025) found that ___

    Our results are similar to Johnson et al in terms of ___

    However, they differ because ___

9. Repeat steps 7 and 8 by commenting on your other findings.

10. One or two sentences on what your results mean.

Think about at which steps you would begin a new paragraph.

5.8 Exercises (cont.)

English for Academic Research: Writing Exercises

> Explaining figures and tables: 4.19
>
> Highlighting your findings: 8.6–8.8
>
> Structure: 10.7

English for Academic Research: Grammar Exercises

> Articles (a, the): 22.1, 22.2
>
> Active vs passive: 22.3
>
> Tenses: 22.4

English for Academic Research: Vocabulary Exercises

> Useful phrases: 8.8, 8.11, 8.12

100 Typical Mistakes

> 3.20–3.24

English for Writing Research Papers

> Clarifying what you did and what others did: Chapter 7
>
> Highlighting your findings: Chapter 8
>
> Writing the Results section: Chapter 17

Chapter 6
Discussion Part 1

6.1 What is a Discussion?

1) When you have just watched a movie with some friends, or when you are discussing a book that you have all read, which of the following do you do?

- discuss what you think the director / author was trying to do (i.e. the aim of the movie / book)

- say which parts of the movie / book you liked the best and why

- analyse the strengths and weaknesses

- discuss why certain characters behaved in a particular way

- in movies, talk about the performance of the actors

- discuss how the movie was shot / discuss the style of the book

- compare the movie / book with others by the same director / author

2) Can you see any connection between discussions about movies and books, and the Discussion section in a paper?

Imagine that you have just finished watching your favorite science fiction movie with some new friends who had never seen the movie before. When you've turned off the screen, you begin discussing the movie together.

1. You *highlight* your favorite bits in the movie for your friends and explain why you like these bits. You also explain why these bits are important to the film and how they fit in with other movies that i) the director has made, ii) cover similar ground or use a similar technique (maybe a similar plot, setting, pace, camerawork).

2. You discuss the *performances* of the main actors, and perhaps discuss these performances in relation to previous performances in other movies starring the same actors.

© The Author(s), under exclusive license to Springer Nature
Switzerland AG 2022
A. Wallwork, *Writing an Academic Paper in English*, English for Academic
Research, https://doi.org/10.1007/978-3-030-95615-8_6

6.1 What is a Discussion? (cont.)

3. Your friends say they had some difficulty understanding the plot at times, and didn't really understand who was who. You *differentiate more in detail the roles of the main characters*, so that your friends can understand better which characters in the movie *did what and why*.

4. One of your friends then confesses that she felt the film was too long and that there was only one scene with special effects and those effects were not very good. You *explain that although* the movie is long it is no longer than other movies of the same type and that in any case its length *is also justified by x, y and z*. With regard to the special effects, you explain that the movie only had a low budget, and that *in any case* it doesn't matter that the effects were not very good because p, q and r.

5. Your friends suggest that *in the future* you all go and see a movie by another director.

The Discussion in a paper has strong similarities with points 1, 2 and 4 above, and also has relation to points 3 and 5. In fact, in the Discussion you:

1. *highlight* for the reader the main results of your research and compare your results with what others in the literature have done / found

2. discuss how well your instrumentation / model / hypothesis performed, and compare this *performance* with others in the literature

3. clearly *differentiate* at all times what YOU found vs what OTHERS found

4. admit the *limitations* of your research and, where possible, justify them (you only had a small budget, small sample, limited time, and *in any case* others in the fields have had the same difficulty, even authors who have been published by the same journal where you wish to published)

5. talk about what you (or the community in general) will or might do *in the future*

6.2   How should I interpret my figures, tables and results?

1. Look again at the papers you analysed in Section 5.4.

2. Quickly read the Abstract and Introduction.

3. Look at the figures and tables. Decide how you would <u>interpret</u> the information contained in them. Write some notes in answer to the questions below.

   • What are the key data? What do they really mean in relation to the author's aims set out in the Abstract and Introduction?

   • What data, if any, do not appear to support what the author expected to find?

4. Now read the Discussion. Compare your notes with what the authors wrote.

5. Finally, answer the following questions:

   • How did the author organize the Discussion?

   • How long were the paragraphs?

   • Was each table and figure commented on individually, or were they grouped together for commentary?

   • Did the author mention any limitations of their study?

6. Note down any useful phrases that the author used to highlight their findings.

The rest of this chapter and the next chapter expand on what you have learned from the exercise above.

84

6.3 What strategies can I use to highlight my main findings and their importance?

1. Do you know what 'highlight' means? What do you think might be the origin of this word?

2. Do you use highlighter pens when you read a printed text? What kind of things do you highlight?

3. When you want to make a sentence or paragraph in your text stand out for your readers, which of the following techniques do you use:

    underlining

    words and phrases in **bold** or *italics*

    CAPITAL letters

    bullet points (•)

    background color

borders

    using lots of white space (i.e. one line space between paragraphs)

    short sentences

    short paragraphs

4. Which of the above can you use in an academic paper?

1) The word 'highlight' was originally used to indicate the "brightest part of a subject" in a painting, i.e. the part that the painter wanted viewers to notice the most. Below is a light that is high: it is used in theaters to focus on a particular actor or musician.

6.3 What strategies can I use to highlight my main findings and their importance? (cont.)

The word 'highlights' is used in the academic world to indicate the main points of a paper.

2) Using a highlighter pen helps you to identify the most relevant parts in a text. You can then review what you have highlighted and ignore the other parts of the text.

3) Most journals allow very little formatting of the text, so the first seven formatting options above are rarely used. This is unfortunate, as bullets and white space make a text more immediately understandable. However, you <u>can</u> use short sentences and paragraphs.

Now turn to the next page. Visually, what effect does it have on you? Note: You do <u>not</u> need to read it.

6.3 What strategies can I use to highlight my main findings and their importance? (cont.)

This is one ridiculously long paragraph containing all kinds of information about everything that you can possibly imagine and conceive. This is one ridiculously long paragraph containing all kinds of information about everything that you can possibly imagine and conceive. Here are my findings you will be lucky if you can see them here buried in the midst of this ridiculously long paragraph containing all kinds of information about everything that you can possibly imagine and conceive. And now I will continue with this ridiculously long paragraph containing all kinds of information about everything that you can possibly imagine and conceive. So here we go again with this ridiculously long paragraph containing all kinds of information about everything that you can possibly imagine and conceive. This is one ridiculously long paragraph containing all kinds of information about everything that you can possibly imagine and conceive. This is one ridiculously long paragraph containing all kinds of information about everything that you can possibly imagine and conceive. This is one ridiculously long paragraph containing all kinds of information about everything that you can possibly imagine and conceive. Here are my findings you will be lucky if you can see them here buried in the midst of this ridiculously long paragraph containing all kinds of information about everything that you can possibly imagine and conceive. And now I will continue with this ridiculously long paragraph containing all kinds of information about everything that you can possibly imagine and conceive. So here we go again with this ridiculously long paragraph containing all kinds of information about everything that you can possibly imagine and conceive. This is one ridiculously long paragraph containing all kinds of information about everything that you can possibly imagine and conceive. This is one ridiculously long paragraph containing all kinds of information about everything that you can possibly imagine and conceive. This is one ridiculously long paragraph containing all kinds of information about everything that you can possibly imagine and conceive. Here are my findings you will be lucky if you can see them here buried in the midst of this ridiculously long paragraph containing all kinds of information about everything that you can possibly imagine and conceive. And now I will continue with this ridiculously long paragraph containing all kinds of information about everything that you can possibly imagine and conceive. So here we go again with this ridiculously long paragraph containing all kinds of information about everything that you can possibly imagine and conceive. This is one ridiculously long paragraph containing all kinds of information about everything that you can possibly imagine and conceive. This is one ridiculously long paragraph containing all kinds of information about everything that you can possibly imagine and conceive. Here are my findings you will be lucky if you can see them here buried in the midst of this ridiculously long paragraph containing all kinds of information about everything that you can possibly imagine and conceive. And now I will continue with this ridiculously long paragraph containing all kinds of information about everything that you can possibly imagine and conceive. So here we go again with this ridiculously long paragraph containing all kinds of information about everything that you can possibly imagine and conceive. This is one ridiculously long paragraph containing all kinds of information about everything that you can possibly imagine and conceive. This is one ridiculously long paragraph containing all kinds of information about everything that you can possibly imagine and conceive. This is one ridiculously long paragraph containing all kinds of information about everything that you can possibly imagine and conceive. Here are my findings you will be lucky if you can see them here buried in the midst of this ridiculously long paragraph containing all kinds of information about everything that you can possibly imagine and conceive. And now I will continue with this ridiculously long paragraph containing all kinds of information about everything that you can possibly imagine and conceive. So here we go again with this ridiculously long paragraph containing all kinds of information about everything that you can possibly imagine and conceive. This is one ridiculously long paragraph containing all kinds of information about everything that you can possibly imagine and conceive. This is one ridiculously long paragraph containing all kinds of information about everything that you can possibly imagine and conceive. This is one ridiculously long paragraph containing all kinds of information about everything that you can possibly imagine and conceive. Here are my findings you will be lucky if you can see them here buried in the midst of this ridiculously long paragraph containing all kinds of information about everything that you can possibly imagine and conceive. And now I will continue with this ridiculously long paragraph containing all kinds of information about everything that you can possibly imagine and conceive. So here we go again with this ridiculously long paragraph containing all kinds of information about everything that you can possibly imagine and conceive. This is one ridiculously long paragraph containing all kinds of information about everything that you can possibly imagine and conceive.

6.3 What strategies can I use to highlight my main findings and their importance? (cont.)

When you see a text like the one on the previous page, are you encouraged to read it? Or would you rather skip it because it is hard on your eyes (and brain) to read?

If you want readers to read what you have written, you have to make it easy for them VISUALLY, not just conceptually and linguistically.

When you have a key finding and you want to ensure that your readers can see it and read it, then use short sentences in a short paragraph. However, don't use short sentences and short paragraphs throughout the entire paper: i) the effect will be lost as they will not stand out from the rest of the text, ii) some reviewers and editors may think it is bad style (it isn't bad style, as long as it serves a good purpose).

Another way to highlight something is to use certain words that attract the reader's attention. You can use certain link words to do this (e.g. *however, in contrast, on the other hand* – see 6.3) and adverbs such as *interestingly, counterintuitively*. The key point is that these words don't take up too much space. So rather than saying *It is worthwhile noting that* or *It should be highlighted that*, simply write *Note that*.

Often you can achieve the same effect simply by beginning a new paragraph.

Analyse the Discussion of a paper you have written or one you have found in a journal. Highlight:

- sentences that are too long and would be clearer if divided into shorter sentences
- places where a long paragraph could be divided into two or more shorter paragraphs

To learn more about how to structure paragraphs and sentences see Chapter 3 (Structuring Paragraphs) and Chapter 4 (Breaking Up Long Sentences) in *English for Writing Research Papers*. You can find exercises in Chapter 3 of *English for Writing Academic Research: Writing Exercises*.

6.4 How should I compare the performance of a test, device etc in my study with the performance of similar test, device etc in another researcher's study?

Compare ONE of the following:

- your country's climate vs Norway's or Brazil's
- your lifestyle and values vs your parents' lifestyle and values
- the music / movies / books you like now vs the ones you liked 5–10 years ago
- your university faculty vs another faculty
- (your) life pre-virus pandemics and pre-climate change catastrophes vs (your) life pre-Covid vs (your) vs (your) life now
- dogs vs cats

Which of the following link words did you use? Link words are words that connect one phrase to another to highlight the logical progression of an argument.

> about, as far as … is concerned, with regard to, regarding
>
> also, in addition, further, furthermore, moreover
>
> because, why, due to, for, insofar as, owing to, since
>
> both, either, neither
>
> even if, even though, although
>
> the former, the latter
>
> however, although, but, yet, despite
>
> instead, on the other hand, whereas, on the contrary
>
> thus, therefore, hence, consequently, so

To learn how link words are used see Chapter 8 (Link Words) in the companion volume *Grammar, Usage and Strategies*. In the same book see Chapter 5 (Comparisons).

You can find exercises on using Link Words in Chapter 4 *English for Writing Academic Research: Writing Exercises*, and Chapter 2 *English for Writing Academic Research: Vocabulary Exercises*.

6.4 How should I compare the performance of a test, device etc in my study with the performance of similar test, device etc in another researcher's study? (cont.)

Choose another topic from the topics listed at the beginning of this section. Imagine you are writing an academic report.

When you have finished, note which of link words you used. If you deleted them, would the reader still understand?

Link words are very useful for connecting ideas into a logical thread. Unfortunately, they tend to be overused, particularly by researchers who try to introduce an apparent logical structure into a text where in reality there is no logical structure.

Your text should be reasonably clear even without link words. However, words and phrases like *thus, on the other hand, however* and *because* (and all similar words) are generally very useful as they alert readers to a consequence or to a possible change in point of view. Others, such as *in addition,* can become very tedious if overused.

6.5 How can I make it clear when I am discussing my results and not the results of another author?

Imagine you are comparing your exam results with a friend's exam results, or your study with a friend's study. In your first paragraph which would you write?

> *My results were not as good as my friend's results.* or ***The** results were not as ...*

> *My study showed that ...* or ***The** study showed that ...* or ***This** study showed that ...*

In the Discussion section (and generally speaking in all the paper) the easiest way to differentiate what you did and found from what another author in the literature did and found is to use personal pronouns: *we* and *our*.

Using *we* (*we studied*) and *our* (*our study*) avoids ambiguity. The reader does not have to make a mental effort to understand whose method or results are being discussed. Unfortunately, in some disciplines there is a bias against using personal pronouns, and passive forms are used instead. However, the passive is often ambiguous, e.g. *a test was carried out to do xyz* – who carried out the test: the author of the paper or another author?

Not clearly differentiating your work from another author's work is possibly the biggest reason for confusion for the reader in academic writing. To learn more about this extremely important aspect, see Chapter 7 *Clarifying Who Did What* in English for Writing Research Papers.

6.5   How can I make it clear when I am discussing my results and not the results of another author? (cont.)

Below is an extract from a totally fictitious paper written by Smith et al. Look at the words and phrases in **bold [1–6]**. In each case decide if it is IMMEDIATELY 100% clear whose research is being referred to: a) Smith's b) another author's. By 'immediately' I mean you understand when you read the verb without having to read the entire sentence.

No significant difference in the prevalence rates of different types of selfish behaviors have been highlighted in relation either to the time of day or to the season of the year (Temporanda et al. 2022). **[1] In this study,** the time of day was divided into six-hour intervals, as also suggested by Kronos et al. (2021). In addition, subjects who drove dangerously and put their passengers at risk **[2] showed** this behavior both in spring and autumn, in line with Wagen et al. (2022). Data stratified per sex and age **[3] have shown** a significantly higher prevalence of selfish behaviors in men aged between 18 and 23, as reported in another survey (Andras et al., 2023), confirming that men feel less responsibility for others than women. **[4] Results obtained** show that younger women (≤30 years) had lower tolerance for the actions of others than older women. Similar results were also reported in Canada, Saudi Arabia and the Republic of Ireland (Donna et al., 2022; Alnisa et al., 2019; Bean et al., 2024). Significant variations in the prevalence rates **[5] were also found by the authors** in subjects from Japan and Korea, and this is in accordance with findings reported by Yeoseong (2026) and Otoko et al (2024). **[6] In this survey** it has been also found that a further important factor is related to the type of questionnaire used in assessing behaviors.

1) NOT CLEAR *In this study* is confusing as it initially it seems like the reference is to Temporada (the author referenced in the previous study), though in reality it refers to Smith's study.

Clear solution: *In our study …*

2) CLEAR If the reader understands that *In this study* refers to Smith's study, then it will be clear that *showed* refers to Smith's results.

3) NOT CLEAR *have shown* is the PRESENT PERFECT which generally refers to some action at some non-specified time in the past. So the reader is initially confused regarding which data (Smith's or another author's) is being referred to.

Clear solution: *When we stratified our date by sex and age, this revealed a significantly higher ….*

6.5 How can I make it clear when I am discussing my results and not the results of another author? (cont.)

4) NOT CLEAR *Results obtained* – we cannot immediately know whose results these are.

Clear solution: *Our results show ...*

5) NOT CLEAR *were also found by the authors* – which authors? The use of the passive form means that there is no subject to the verb. The previous sentence has mentioned the work of other authors, so it is not immediately clear whether Smith *found* something or another author.

Clear solution: *We also found significant ...*

6) NOT CLEAR *In this survey* – this is a similar problem to Point (1). The previous sentence ended with a reference to Otoko (another author), so we might think that the *survey* refers to Otoko's work. It is also confusing because i) the PRESENT PERFECT is used (see Point 3); ii) Smith has used the term *survey* to describe his work, whereas previously he used *study*, so the reader might think that the *survey* and the *study* are two different things.

Clear solution: *In our study we also found that ...*

✐

Read the Discussion section in some papers from a journal in your field. Each time a finding/result is mentioned, decide if it is clear if this is what the author of the paper that are you are reading found or the author of another paper. If it is not clear, think of how the author could have made it clearer.

6.6 Why is it important to admit the limitations of my study?

What would you do in the following situations?

1. A new friend asks you to go hiking in the mountains. You are afraid of heights.

2. You are offered a place on a fantastic summer school course. The school requires you to have knowledge of w, x, y and z. You have no knowledge of w.

3. Several years ago you spent an academic year in France, which you have mentioned on your CV. Your professor, who has read your CV, asks you to do a presentation in French at a conference in France. You have forgotten nearly all of the little French you learned during your exchange year.

4. A potential new boy / girlfriend who you are really interested in impressing, asks you to go dancing. You are uncoordinated and have no sense of rhythm. However, previously you have told this person that you love dancing.

We all have limitations. Sometimes it is difficult to be honest and transparent about them, even though the consequences are never usually as bad as we think. We also tend to appreciate other people when they are honest and transparent with us.

Almost certainly there are weaknesses in your research – in your methods, in the results, in your interpretation of the results. If you don't mention them, then the reviewers of the paper probably will. There is then a chance that your paper will be rejected (in the same way as your new partner might reject you!). In the best possible scenario the referees and editor will ask you to write an explanation of your limitations in a revised version of your paper.

Instead, if you are transparent about your limitations in your first draft of the paper, there is a greater chance that your paper will be accepted more quickly.

And the great news is that you can talk about these limitations when you do any oral presentations of your research. You can then hope that someone in the audience may be able to give you some suggestions on how to overcome such limitations (not during your presentation itself, but later during the social dinner).

Science is as much about failures as successes. Acknowledging limits is how science progresses.

6.6 Why is it important to admit the limitations of my study? (cont.)

Limitations do not, of course, always regard yourself and your own work, but also the limitations that you have found in other researcher's work. Treat these other authors and reviewers in a positive way and with respect. If you adopt an aggressive or very critical approach, your reviewers and readers will not respect you and you will lose some credibility as a scientist.

Note: In some journals the limitations are mentioned in the Conclusions rather than the Discussion. In any case, try not to end the Discussion or Conclusions with your limitations. Instead, mention them in the penultimate paragraph, and focus on the positive aspects of your work in the final paragraph. You want readers to finish your paper thinking about the benefits of your research rather than its problems.

6.7 How can I justify my limitations?

Which of the following are true for you in relation to your current research project?

a) You don't have sufficient time to carry out all the tests you need to do.

b) Old data – you need more recent data.

c) You don't have access to particular libraries, data, equipment, etc.

d) Your sample size is too small or too restricted.

e) You don't have sufficient funds.

f) You don't have the right tools, substances, equipment.

g) So far you've only done *in vitro* tests, you need to do *in vivo* tests.

Below are some possible ways to talk about such limitations in your paper. What strategy do they all have in common?

a) The results presented in this paper have focused on testing x and y. We are currently also testing z, and our results will be published in a separate paper.

b) Currently we only have data for up to three years ago. In fact, to the best of our knowledge more recent data has not been compiled. In any case, the data for the last twenty years seem to be following the same trend. Thus it seems likely that this trend has been in force for the last three years as well. We plan to verify this when the new data become available.

c) Given where we are located and the small size of our institute, we do not have direct access to the xyz libraries. However, most of the works contained in the xyz libraries are available as Google Books, which we used as one of our sources of data collection.

d) Our research was confined to pqr. However, future research needs to include xyz. We hope that other researchers will take up this call and begin investigating xyz.

e) As many other authors have found, this kind of research is expensive [Smith et al, 2022; Chan 2023, Sakamoto, 2026]. To further our studies, we are currently looking for collaborators to create a joint working group to solve this vital issue.

6.7 How can I justify my limitations? (cont.)

f) Although we used an x rather than a y, this is actually a common issues in our field and past studies have overcome it by adopting the same approach as us [May et al, 2024; Kant 2025, Maight 2026, Cud 2027].

g) So far we have only been unable to carry out *in vitro* tests. We are thus planning to carry out *in vivo* tests in order to confirm the results of our *in vitro* tests.

The strategy is:

1. admit the problem

2. where possible, show that the problem is common (i.e. other authors have had the same difficulty)

3. provide a solution – i.e. say what you plan to do to overcome the problem

Think about the things that other people (your professor, parents, friends) have criticized you for.

Write about these limitations, or invent them if you prefer, and justify them.

6.8   How should I write about my limitations?

In the extract below from a Discussion, the authors discuss the limitations of their research, plus lines of future research. Answer the questions:

a) In Paragraph 1, how does the author use Hamonija's study to justify the limitation of their own study?

b) In Paragraph 2, what is the purpose of the word *unfortunately*?

c) What is the purpose of Paragraph 3? [NB: This info is typically given either in the Discussion or in the Conclusions].

PARA 1 Although our research was wide reaching, it did not include investigations into egg-breaking habits shown by citizens in South America or the entire continent of Africa. Hamonija's study (2026) on the correlation between egg breaking and musical taste also neglected these two continents, but the authors conducted a series of mini surveys in Bolivia and Botswana and found that the results confirmed the results of their overall study.

PARA 2 Another possible limitation of our study was that the researchers were, coincidentally, all small-enders, i.e. they all break their eggs at the small end. This may have meant that they unintentionally looked for negative behaviors in big-enders, and ignored the same negative behaviors in small-enders. Unfortunately, it seems unlikely that a group of big-ender researchers would be interested in investigating the phenomenon of selfishness. In fact, big-enders would seem to have a lack of general empathy or sense of community, but tend to focus on achieving their own goals at the expense of others.

PARA 3 Finally, we believe that our results give important insights into why a much lower percentage of big-enders play sports where an individual excels rather than a team, as this would seem to indicate a direct link with promoting their ego. This correlation between egg-breaking and the ego has so far only been investigated in the US and the UK (Gitz & Tosa, 2023) and would certainly be an avenue for future research in other parts of the world.

a) The idea is that i) you admit you have a limitation, ii) you try to justify it (in this case by saying someone else had a similar problem). To understand why it is important to talk about limitations see 6.5 and 6.6.

b) Any adverb placed at the beginning of a sentence or paragraph and which is separated by a comma (,) attracts the eye of the reader. It is designed to act like a signpost, telling the reader what to expect in the rest of the sentence.

6.8 How should I write about my limitations? (cont.)

c) If the Discussion and Conclusions are in a single section, then a paragraph like Paragraph 3 is needed to: i) highlight again the overall importance of your research, ii) outline what you (or others in the field) could do in the future to enhance the knowledge of the topic.

Use one or more strategies above and outline some of the limitations of your current research or your research field in general, and how these limits are being overcome. You can adapt some of the typical phrases from the next chapter (see 7.6)

To learn more about dealing with limitations see 10.5 in the companion volume *Giving an Academic Presentation in English*.

English for Academic Research: Writing Exercises

    Anticipating possible objections: 9.1

    Indicating level of certainty: 9.2–9.4

    Discussing limitations: 9.5–9.9

    Hedging: 9.10–9.15

English for Writing Research Papers

    Differentiating your findings from other authors' findings: Chapter 7

    Highlighting your findings: Chapter 8

    Discussing your limitations: Chapter 9

    Hedging and criticizing: Chapter 10

    Plagiarizing and paraphrasing: Chapter 11

    Writing the Discussion: Chapter 18

Chapter 7
Discussion Part 2

7.1 Discussion Model: Part 1

In a Discussion you compare your results with other similar research in the literature and discuss the implications. You should also talk about the limitations of methods and results and work in general.

Below is a short version of a Discussion section, excluding a discussion of limitations (see 7.2). In their research the authors investigated various selfish behaviors in relation to *egg endedness*, i.e. whether someone breaks an egg at the big end or the small end.

I have divided the text into six paragraphs (1–3 are examined in this subsection, and 4–6 in the next subsection: 7.2). Read the first three paragraphs and answer the questions below.

PARA 1 We investigated a series of selfish behaviors to understand whether they are more frequently shown by big-enders (BEs) and small-enders (SEs), and what the consequent implications are on community living. We also compared these behaviors with right-handers and left-handers, i.e. people with a propensity to use one hand rather than the other to break their eggs.

PARA 2 Other authors have studied selfish behavior of BEs and SEs in relation to level of income (Dosh et al, 2020), level of education and critical thinking (Schule et al, 2019), intelligence quotient and cognitive dissonance (Iqbal & Mensa, 2025), musical taste (Hamonija, 2026), taste in movies (Flix & Odeon, 2027), and historical tyrants (Des Pott et al, 2028). However, in all cases the sample sizes were relatively small – education (501 subjects), IQ (145), music (88), movies (345), and tyrants (29).

PARA 3 Our sample was approximately 10,000 people spread over three continents (N. America, Europe and Asia). In fact, to the best of our knowledge our sample is the largest ever used in a psycho-social study of endedness, where 'endedness' is defined as the tendency to break an egg at one end more frequently than the other end.

© The Author(s), under exclusive license to Springer Nature   99
Switzerland AG 2022
A. Wallwork, *Writing an Academic Paper in English*, English for Academic
Research, https://doi.org/10.1007/978-3-030-95615-8_7

7.1 Discussion Model: Part 1 (cont.)

Which of the following do the authors of the paper do?

a) differentiate between their own work and that of other people's work

b) use *we / our* to describe their own work, and use the name of the relevant author(s) to describe other people's work

c) highlight the main disadvantage of previous work done in their field

d) use adjectives to highlight the importance of their work

e) use the adverb *however* to indicate that they are about to say something that is in contrast to what they have just said

f) use the phrase *to the best of our knowledge* in case in reality there are others in the field who have done something similar

The authors use all the strategies except for (d). Adjectives are often redundant or misleading in academic texts. Rather than saying something is *interesting* or *important*, explain how/why it is interesting or important. Instead of saying *a large number of*, try to give a more precise number – what is large for you, may be small for your reader.

7.2 Discussion Model: Part 2

✎

Paragraphs 4–6 compare the author's findings and other findings in the literature (which the authors have also cited in their Introduction). Read and then answer the questions below.

PARA 4 Our results confirmed nearly all the results in the literature cited above. In line with Dosh (2020), who found that the higher the income the more likelihood of being big-enders (BEs), we found that those who frequently broke the speed limit on the highway were driving expensive cars to match their big egos. Schule (2019) found that critical thinking was less evident in BEs. This was confirmed in our study by the lack of empathy shown by BEs in our study: they were unable to make the connection between playing loud music at night and keeping the neighbors awake.

PARA 5 Interestingly, a study (Des Pott et al, 2028) on historical tyrants and criminals found no difference between big-enders (e.g. Ghenghis Khan, Jack the Ripper, Stalin) and small-enders (Hitler and Attila the Hun). Their findings (Des Pott et al, 2028) conflict with our results, as we found a far higher number of semi-criminal selfish behaviors (dropping litter, double parking) associated with big-enders.

PARA 6 The most similar study to ours is certainly Flix & Odeon's (2027) who, like us, found that movies with a high element of violence were preferred by BEs. They also found that movies with negative portrayals of women and ethnic groups tended to be enjoyed more by BEs than SEs. Our study did not investigate women and ethnic groups, and nor did it investigate the levels of selfishness showed by men as opposed to women – we plan to differentiate between men and women in a future work.

✎

Answer the questions:

a) The majority of verbs (both those referring to the present paper and to the literature) are in the PAST SIMPLE – why?

b) Why is the PRESENT SIMPLE used in the two cases below?

   i) *Their findings conflict with our results.*

   ii) *We plan to differentiate between genders in a future work.*

c) In which of the above two sentences, could the PRESENT SIMPLE be replaced by the PRESENT CONTINUOUS – why?

d) What function does *Interestingly* play at the beginning of Paragraph 5?

e) What is the purpose of Paragraph 6?

7.2 Discussion Model: Part 2 (cont.)

Below I have used the word *you* to indicate the authors of the paper. This enables me to distinguish *you* the author of the paper from other authors of other papers.

a) The PAST SIMPLE is used in the Results to describe what you did in your research. The research reported in the paper is finished and took place at a precise time in the past, i.e. before you began writing your manuscript. The results in the literature were also the outcome of experiments conducted in the past. An exception to this rule is highlighted in the sentence *Other authors have studied selfish behavior in relation to level of income.* The PRESENT PERFECT is used here because it indicates a series of actions that began in the past, are continuing now in the present, and are likely to continue into the future. This is because the topic of big-enders vs small-enders is still open. Other researchers will study it in the future. However, when you mention specific studies (e.g. *Schule (2019) found that …*) you need the PAST SIMPLE particularly as a precise date is mentioned (2019).

b, c) *Their findings conflict with our results.* You are not talking about something that happened in the past, but you are making an interpretation now in the paper. It is fundamental to distinguish between what you did in the lab (all in the past) and what you are doing now while writing the paper (PRESENT SIMPLE, and sometimes PRESENT PERFECT).

We plan to differentiate between men and women in a future work. The plan is a future plan. You could also say: *We are planning to* but *We plan* sounds more formal and is thus more appropriate. The meaning however is the same.

d) Particularly if placed at the beginning of a new paragraph, *interestingly* attracts the attention of the reader, who will want to know what exactly is interesting. It is a good device for regaining your readers' attention. Words with a similar function are *counterintuitively* and *unexpectedly*. However, you should use such words just once or twice in your entire paper, otherwise they lose their power of attraction. Also, as stated in 7.1, avoid adjectives if it would be more helpful for the reader to understand WHY something is *important* or *interesting*, instead of just merely stating that it is *important* or *interesting*.

e) The aim of Paragraph 6 is to cite another study with similar findings to yours, but which also found something that you did not find. This then leads logically into Paragraph 7 which introduces some of the limitations of your study.

7.3 A revision of all tenses plus those typically used in the Discussion

PRESENT SIMPLE

PRESENT SIMPLE to describe to what your findings reveal or to talk in general. It is also used with verbs such as *believe, feel, propose, advocate* when you are talking about your opinions.

> We have shown, for what **we believe** is the first time, that there **is** a link between ...

> Selfish behaviors **are** considerably more prevalent in ...

PRESENT SIMPLE is also used to:

* describe facts that are part of the public domain.

> Newton's law of gravitation **states** that ...

> Smoking **is known** to cause cancer ...

> Analysis of variance **is** a statistical method in which the variation in a set of observation **is divided** into ...

* envisage future scenarios

> We thus **advocate** a form of wise government where citizens **are encouraged** to think about the general welfare of their fellow citizens.

PRESENT PERFECT (HAVE + PAST PARTICIPLE)

The PRESENT PERFECT is used when:

* describing a situation that began in the past and continues into the present (first and second examples below), or which began in the past and has consequences now (third example)

> England **has been** a democracy since the People Acts of 1918 and 1928 gave the vote to all men and women over the age of 21. *England continues to be a democracy.*

> Several papers **have been written** on this topic (James 2018, Williams 2021, Jones 2026). *Research in this area is still in progress.*

> The capitalist model **has led** to a society in which ...

7.3 A revision of all tenses plus those typically used in the Discussion (cont.)

- informing the reviewers of your paper what changes you have made from the original version that you sent the journal

> We **have added** two new tables. We **have restructured** the Introduction. We **have corrected** the typos in lines 45, 89 and 156.

In the Conclusions, use the PRESENT PERFECT to describe what you have done in the paper itself (i.e. NOT during the actual research process, but during the writing process).

> We **have shown** a link between selfish behavior and egg-breaking habits.

PAST SIMPLE

Use the PAST SIMPLE to refer to your results.

> We **found** that big-enders *tended* to be more selfish, and thus less community minded, than small-enders.

In the above example, the authors could have written *tended to be*. Using the present (*tend*) gives a sense of greater certainty. The past (*tended*) means exclusively what the authors found in their research but which may not necessarily be generalizable.

- The PAST SIMPLE is also used to talk about past events.

> Jonathan Swift **wrote** Gulliver's Travels in 1726.

PAST PERFECT

PAST PERFECT This tense is quite rare in academic papers. Use it when you want readers to understand that one action had been concluded before another action began.

> After the samples **had been immersed** in water for 24 hours, they were then dried.

The sentence above could be rephrased as:

> The samples **were immersed** in water for 24 hours. They were then dried.

7.3 A revision of all tenses plus those typically used in the Discussion (cont.)

Here are some more examples:

Swift **wrote** *Gulliver's Travels*.

Swift **wrote** *An Argument against Abolishing Christianity* before he **wrote** *Gulliver's Travels*.

Swift **had already written** more than ten books before he wrote *Gulliver's Travels*.

In the first sentence, there is only one past action, so only the past simple (*wrote*) is possible. In the second, we are talking about a sequence of separate past actions – both tenses are possible in the first verb, but the past simple is more appropriate if we just want to list events in chronological order. In the third, the past perfect (*had written*) gets the reader to notice that one event happened before another – we are not interested so much in the sequence but perhaps in the (surprising) relationship between events (as highlighted by the use of *already*).

WILL

The future form, *will*, is rarely used in academic papers. In fact, in your paper you are generally talking about what you did (completed) in your research, rather than what you will do in the future. In any case, in the Conclusions *will* can used to refer to future work or to make predictions.

Future work **will involve** investigating x, y and z.

WOULD AND CONDITIONAL FORMS

In English there are four types of CONDITIONAL form. None of these forms are commonly used in scientific papers. I am reporting them here as they are nevertheless commonly used on other occasions. Conditional sentences are often made up of two parts. The two parts can be inverted.

ZERO CONDITIONAL (if + present + present) – statements that are always true

If black paint **is mixed** with white this **produces** grey.

FIRST CONDITIONAL (if + present + will) – a possible / probable future event and its consequences

If people **take** the vaccine, they **will be protected** for up to one year.

If you **do not make** the suggested modifications, then your paper **will not be accepted**.

7.3 A revision of all tenses plus those typically used in the Discussion (cont.)

SECOND CONDITIONAL (if + past + would) – hypothetical situations that are quite unlikely to happen

> If people **learned** to stop acting selfishly, then positive daily behaviors **would** then **become** entrenched in society.

THIRD CONDITIONAL (if + had + past participle, + would have + past participle) – refers to situations that had the potential to happen but in reality did not happen

> If you **had studied** English at school, this **would have helped** you pass the English test last year.

CAN, MAY, COULD, MIGHT

In the Discussion you interpret your results, but sometimes you are not 100% confident of what your results really mean. In this case you can use words (known as modal verbs) such as *can, may, could,* and *might* (see Chapter 3 in *Grammar, Usage and Strategies*).

Below are some very simplified rules.

can indicates a characteristic behavior – we know that this behavior happens. *may* indicates only the potential for something to happen. It indicates uncertainty and is thus used to make hypotheses, to speculate about a probability. If the probability refers to something in the past, them *may* + *have* + past participle is used – do <u>not</u> use *can* in such cases.

> Bilinguals are people that **can** speak two languages.

> Government cuts in education funding **can** have devastating effects on research (Refs. 12–28).

> In the next decade such government cuts **may** lead to the closure of several universities.

> The sample **may** have been contaminated by residues.

cannot (+ *have* + past participle) indicates impossibility (i.e. a certain event or scenario is not possible)

may not (+ *have* + past participle) indicates there is a possibility that something will not happen (i.e. a certain event or scenario is not likely)

> Swift was not born until 1667, so this work (dated 1660) **cannot** have been written by him.

> Although our sample was only small, this **may not** have affected the results because the sample was, in any case, very representative.

7.3 A revision of all tenses plus those typically used in the Discussion (cont.)

could in the affirmative indicates a regular past ability, i.e. something that someone or something was able to do regularly; *was able to* can also be used in this context. However, when describing an ability to do something on one particular past occasion, do not use *could*. Instead, use a form of *to be able to, to succeed in* or *to manage*

> The patient **could / was able to** walk at the age of six months.

> The patient **was not able to walk** for six months after the operation.

> We **managed / were able to** finish the manuscript on time. = We **succeeded** in finishing the ...

> NO! ~~We could finish the manuscript on time so we met the deadline.~~

could is often used to suggest a possible course of action. *might* indicates a possible reaction to or consequence of a course of action – but there is no certainty that this reaction or consequence will take place. The difference is very subtle and not always clear.

> Future research **could** be directed towards elucidating this pathology. Such research **might** then reveal the true causes of this pathology.

> One solution **could** be to get parents and children to swap roles for a day. But what exactly **would / might** happen? How **might** they behave differently?

If you want to practise the various tenses, see these sections in *English for Academic Research: Grammar Exercises.*

present simple and present perfect: Chapter 6

past simple and past perfect: Chapter 7

will: 8.1

conditional forms: Chapter 9

modal verbs: Chapter 12

Use of tenses in the Discussion: Chapter 23

7.4 Typical mistakes made in the Discussion

The Discussion is often the most difficult part of the paper for the reader to understand, especially if the author has failed to distinguish between what he/she did and what others have done.

Check your journal's 'guidelines to authors' to see whether you are permitted to use *we*. If *we* is permitted, then it is relatively easy for you to distinguish between your work and others. Some journals, particularly those regarding Physics, tend to opt for an impersonal form.

If your journal insists on the passive form, you need to be extremely careful. The most important point to remember is that YOU know which is your work and which is someone else's. But the readers do not! You must make it clear for THEM.

7.5 Do's and Don'ts of writing the Discussion

DO ensure that you highlight what your main result reveals compared to what has previously been shown in the literature, or how your main result adds to previous knowledge.

DO ensure that it is very easy for reviewers and readers to:

- identify your contribution
- decide how useful the contribution is
- make a decision about whether this contribution is worth recommending for publication

DO remove any redundant phrases.

DON'T use the term *the authors* to refer to your own work – readers may think you are talking about authors in the literature you have mentioned in the previous sentence.

DON'T forget to put a reference when you are citing other people's work.

For advice on writing clearly and using the minimum number of words see the following chapters in the companion volume *Grammar, Usage and Strategies*:

Chapter 4: Clarity and Empathy

Chapter 9: Paragraphs, Sentence Length, Paraphrasing

7.6   Useful phrases

23 REFERRING BACK TO YOUR RESEARCH AIM

As stated in the Introduction, our main aim / objective / target / purpose / goal *was to ...*

Our research was conducted / undertaken / carried out *in order to ...*

Given that / Since *our main aim was, as mentioned in the Introduction, to ...*

24 MAKING TRANSITIONS, REFERRING TO OTHER PARTS OF THE PAPER

If we now turn to / Turning now to / Let us know look *at the second part ...*

As far *as X is / Xs* are concerned ...

As regards / Regarding / Regarding the use of / As for *X, it was found that ...*

As was mentioned / stated / noted / discussed / reported *in the Methods, ...*

As reported above / previously / earlier / before ...

Please refer to Appendix 2 / Table 6 / the Supplementary Material *for ....*

25 SIGNIFICANT RESULTS AND ACHIEVEMENTS

As expected / anticipated / predicted / forecast / hypothesized, *our experiments* show / demonstrate / prove *that ...*

This finding confirms / points to / highlights / reinforces / validates *the usefulness of X as a ...*

Our experiments confirm / corroborate / are in line with / are consistent with *previous results [Wiley 2009].*

This is in good agreement / in complete agreement / consistent *with ...*

This confirms / supports / lends support to / substantiates *previous findings in the literature ...*

Although / Even though / Despite the fact that *there was some inconsistency ...*

There is satisfactory / good / exceptional / perfect *agreement between ...*

26 OPINIONS AND PROBABILITIES

To the best of our knowledge / As far as we know / We believe that *no other authors have found that x = y.*

Our findings would seem to show / demonstrate / suggest / imply *that x = y.*

We believe that our method could be used / probably be usefully employed *in...*

In our opinion / view, *this method could be used in ...*

7.6 Useful phrases (cont.)

27 RESULTS IN CONTRAST WITH PREVIOUS EVIDENCE

We found that X = 2, whereas / on the other hand *Kamatchi [2021] found that* …

We found much higher values for X than / with respect to *those reported by Pandey [2020].*

Although / Despite the fact that *Li and Mithran [2024] found that X = 2, we found that X = 3.*

In contrast to / contradiction with *earlier findings [Castenas, 2019], we* …

Even though these results differ from some published / previous / earlier *studies (Cossu, 2021; Triana, 2022), they are consistent with those of* …

28 LIMITATIONS

We are aware that our research has two limitations. The first is … The second is … These limitations highlight / reveal / underline / are evidence of *the difficulty of collecting data on* ….

A number of limitations may / might / could have *influenced the results obtained.* First / To begin with … An additional / Another *possible source of error is* …

It was not possible / we were unable *to investigate the significant relationships of X and Y further* because / due to the fact that *Z is* …

Since / Given that / As *the focus of the study was on X* … there is a possibility / there is some likelihood / it is not inconceivable *that dissimilar evaluations would have arisen if the focus had been on Y.*

The restricted use of X could account for / be the reason for / explain why …

There are several sources for / causes of / reasons for *possible error.*

It is very likely / probable / possible *that... and this may have* led to / brought about *changes in* …

This apparent lack of correlation can be attributed to / explained by / justified by …

This happened / occurred / may have happened / may have occurred *because we had not examined X* sufficiently / in enough depth *due to* …

We cannot rule out that X might / may have influenced Y.

The increase in X could be attributed to / might be explained by it / could be interpreted as *being a result of* …

7.7 Exercises

1) Remove the redundancy and rephrase the sentence where necessary, as in the example below.

Research has shown that the reduction of blood cholesterol *can be obtained* by consuming the recommended level of vitamin D (Oranges et al, 2022).

Blood cholesterol can be *reduced* by consuming the recommended level of vitamin D (Oranges et al, 2022).

1. It has been also suggested that egoism may delay growth in children (Kidz et al, 2024).

2. With regard to jumping queues, a range of variability in the propensity to jump queues has been reported in the literature both in big-enders and small-enders (Codex et al, 2021, Line, 2022).

3. Recently, interest in selfish behaviors has increased since these behaviors have been shown to be involved in coronary heart disease [Hart, 2026].

4. Due to their ability to reach the brain, more recently researchers have started to investigate the physiological role of sterols in controlling super-egoism (Me Mi My et al, 2023).

This key indicates what you could potentially remove. Clearly you could remove less (but probably not more). The result is that the text is much quicker for the reader to read, and the sense is more immediate. In examples 1–3 key words are now nearer the beginning of the sentence, i.e. where the reader's eyes tend to focus the most. Grey indicates words that have been removed. Underlining indicates words that have been added.

1. It has been also suggested that egoism may delay growth in children (Kidz et al, 2024).

2. With regard to jumping queues, a range of variability in the propensity to jump queues has been reported in the literature varies both in big-enders and small-enders (Codex et al, 2021, Line, 2022).

3. Recently, interest in selfish behaviors has increased since these behaviors have been shown to be they are involved in coronary heart disease [Hart, 2026].

4. Due to their ability to reach the brain, more recently researchers have started to investigate the physiological role of sterols in controlling super-egoism has been investigated (Me Mi My et al, 2023).

7.7 Exercises (cont.)

2) Look at the beginnings of sentences below. Select which ones you could use in your Discussion. Complete the sentences, modifying them where necessary. Add additional sentences as required.

1. As stated in the Introduction, our main aim was to _____

2. The most striking to emerge from our data / study is that _____

3. We believe that this is the first time that X _____

4. Our technique shows a clear advantage over _____

5. The utility of X / our approach / our method is highlighted by _____

6. These results extend our knowledge of _____

7. Our experiments are in line with previous results [Author, 2024] which showed that _____

8. As suggested by Author [2025], the evidence we found points to _____

9. We found much lower / higher values for _____ than / with respect to those reported by _____

10. Even though our results differ from previous studies (Authors, 2024; Authors, 2025), they are consistent with those of _____ because _____

11. As expected / hypothesized, our experiments show that _____

12. Our findings appear to be well substantiated / supported by _____

13. Our findings would thus seem to demonstrate / imply that _____

14. Our results point to the likelihood / probability that _____

15. We believe that our method could be used employed in _____

3) Using some or all of the sentences you have created in Exercise 2:

- re-state the aim of your research

- briefly summarize your main results

- compare <u>one</u> of your results with others in the literature, highlighting similarities and differences

- state the implications of the result

You can invent whatever information you want, but make sure you follow the structure above and the tenses suggested in this chapter. You can use a personal or an impersonal style (see 2.6 and 9.6) or a mix of the two. You can also adapt phrases from the Useful Phrases section (7.6).

7.7 Exercises (cont.)

English for Academic Research: Writing Exercises

Applications and future work: 9.16

Structure: 10.8, 10.9

English for Academic Research: Grammar Exercises

Tenses: Chapter 23

English for Academic Research: Vocabulary Exercises

Useful phrases: 8.9–8.13

100 Typical Mistakes

Chapter 4

English for Writing Research Papers

Differentiating your findings from other authors' findings: Chapter 7

Highlighting your findings: Chapter 8

Writing the Discussion: Chapter 18

Chapter 8
Conclusions

8.1 What is the purpose of a Conclusions section?

Imagine you are near the end of a job interview. Anna, the interviewer, says: *Before we finish, i) just give me three reasons why we should hire you, ii) one area where you think you might have some weaknesses that you need to improve, and iii) how you see your future.*

a. Would you summarize everything that you have said before, mentioning in chronological order all your experiences (work and study) and what results you obtained from these experiences?

b. What would you do instead?

a) Anna, your interviewer, i) <u>doesn't need</u> all this info, she has heard it earlier in the interview; ii) <u>doesn't have time</u> to hear the whole story again.

b) So what does Anna really want?

1. She wants to know your unique selling points, i.e. what makes you special compared to other candidates. She wants to know what you think the **implications** are of what you have studied and what projects you have done - how these experiences will impact on the work you could do for her company.

2. She is realistic that she will not find the absolute perfect candidate and so she wants to know what areas in your skills you think you need to improve (i.e. **limitations** that you recognize in yourself) so that you can do the best possible job for the institute / company where she works.

3. Anna is also interested in learning how your see your **future** career developing. This will help her decide if it matches the direction of her institute / company.

© The Author(s), under exclusive license to Springer Nature
Switzerland AG 2022

A. Wallwork, *Writing an Academic Paper in English*, English for Academic
Research, https://doi.org/10.1007/978-3-030-95615-8_8

8.1 What is the purpose of a Conclusions section? (cont.)

A Conclusions section covers the same three points above.

1. Discusses the overall meaning and **implications** of the authors' results.

2. Comments on any **limitations** of the study (e.g. in the methodology, in contradictory results, or in the interpretation of the results). However, the limitations may instead be mentioned in the Discussion.

3. Outlines possible paths for **future research**.

Notice that the three points are NOT a summary of the whole paper. You have already summarized your paper in the Abstract.

8.2   What tenses are typically used in the Conclusions?

The Conclusions section below is fictitious, but the case of Birzeit is true (*Peasant Life in the Holy Land*, Rev. C T Wilson, Dutton & Co., 1906).

Find examples of the **tenses and modal verbs** below in the text. Decide why a particular tense was used. See 7.3 for an overview of tenses.

1. present simple active _____

2. present simple passive _____

3. present perfect _____

4. past simple active _____

5. past simple passive _____

6. will _____

7. would _____

8. would have + past participle + past perfect _____

9. might _____

PARA 1 We **(1) have shown**, for what we **(2) believe** is the first time, that there **is** a link between selfish behavior and *endedness*, i.e. whether a person breaks an egg at the big end or the small end. We **(3) found** that big-enders (BEs) tend to be more selfish, and thus less community minded, than small-enders (SEs). This phenomenon **(4) seems** to be true across nations.

PARA 2 Selfish behaviors are considerably more prevalent in the West (US and Europe). This **(5) is highlighted** above all by our finding that BEs have contributed much more to climate change than SEs. It is likely that the current levels of floods and fires **(6) would not have been reached** if the BEs 7) **had followed** the green strategies of the SEs.

PARA 3 In conclusion, we **(8) propose** that in many nations the BE model **(9) has led** to a selfish decadent society where many people **(10) think** only for themselves and not for the good of their community. We thus advocate that policymakers should encourage the general public to think about the general welfare of their fellow citizens. This **(11) would lead** to more social everyday behaviors such as not dropping little, not double parking, and not jumping queues.

8.2   What tenses are typically used in the Conclusions? (cont.)

PARA 4 As future work, we **(12) plan to model / will model** how such policies **(13) might work**. Our inspiration comes from the handling of an outbreak of cholera in Birzeit (Palestine) in the late 19th century. The epidemic came to an end when a village elder ordered the entire population to camp in their vineyards - everyone acted together for the common good under the guidance of wise elders. This case **(14) was reported** by a Christian missionary who noted that "there was no European hand in it ... and it shows what the Fellahin [farmers, agricultural laborers] are capable of under wise and energetic native guidance".

1. present simple active **2, 4, 8, 10** – things that are true now or refer to the present moment

2. present simple passive **5** – refers to something that the reader can see or interpret now

3. present perfect **1** – used to describe what the authors <u>have done</u> in the paper (rather than what they <u>did</u> in their research); **9** – an action from the past to the present that has a consequence now

4. past simple active **3** – refers to what the authors did during their research

5. past simple passive **14** – past action, puts focus on the *case* rather than the *missionary*

6. *will* **12** – *will* tends to indicate certainty about the future, i.e. in this case the authors have probably already planned how to organize their future work. Alternatively *we plan to* is less certain.

7. *would* **11** – to talk hypothetically about a real possibility now or in the future

8. *would have* + past participle + past perfect **6+7** to talk hypothetically about something in the past

9. *might* **13** – hypothetical possibility

Not all Conclusions section are as long as this one. Check with your journal to see:

- the average length
- the structure
- whether the study's limitations are mentioned here or in the Discussion

8.3   How should I structure my Conclusions?

Look at the text in 8.2, which is divided into five paragraphs. What purpose does each paragraph serve?

The text in 8.2 does not mention any limitations to the study (the authors put them in the Discussion). Do you think that limitations are best located in the Discussion or Conclusions?

Para 1: Results (the aim of the study is to see if there is a link between selfish behavior and handedness).

Para 2: Implications.

Para 3: Policy recommendations. Such recommendations tend to be made only in subjects such as political science, social science and economics.

Para 4: Future work.

Use the following 5-step structure to write a short Conclusions section for your paper. You may not need all five steps. The number of sentences you might need for each step is just a suggestion.

1. Aims and results of your paper (2-4 sentences).

2. Limitations (2 sentences) – but only if these limitations are not mentioned in the Discussion.

3. Implications of your results / Highlighting the importance of your research (2-5 sentences) – think in terms of how your results advance on what is already known (in the case of scientific/technical studies), or what governmental policies need to be changed (in the case of social/political sciences and economics), or how your results change current perceptions (in the case of history, art, literature etc).

4. Possible applications of what you have found (2-4 sentences). For example, if you have created a new device, method, or protocol, then state how you think it could be used in practical applications

5. Future work – either what you plan to do yourself, or what you recommend that the research community should do (2 sentences).

See 8.5 for some useful phrases that you can use in your Conclusions.

8.4 Do's and Don'ts of writing the Conclusions

An editorial in *Nature Physics* says this about the Conclusions section:

> Conclusions are not mandatory, and those that merely summarize the preceding results and discussion are unnecessary (and, for publication in *Nature Physics*, will be edited out). Rather, the concluding paragraphs should offer something new to the reader.

DO remember that your Conclusions may be the last section that the referee reads. Consequently, they must be clear and concise, and leave the referee with a good impression.

DON'T just summarize your main findings. Instead remind readers of the most important findings, pointing out how these advance your field from the present state of knowledge.

DO ensure that readers understand how your investigation may have added to the knowledge base in the field.

DO report very clearly why and how these findings may be of interest for future research and applications.

DON'T forget to mention any limitations of your research - unless you have already mentioned the limitations in the Discussion.

DON'T just cut and paste sentences from various other parts of the paper (e.g. the Abstract or the Introduction).

DO provide a strong a clear and high-impact take-home message for your readers.

DO suggest possible avenues for future work (either those that your research team intends to follow or for the scientific community in general), or recommend policy changes (if you are doing research in economics, social sciences, law etc).

DON'T write it in a hurry. Typically, the Conclusions are the last part to be written in a paper and tend to written very fast and without much thought as you are keen to finish the paper and send it to the journal. Instead, the Conclusions need care and attention.

8.5   Useful phrases

29 ANNOUNCING YOUR CONCLUSIONS AND RESTATING THE KEY RESULTS

In conclusion / In summary / In sum / To sum up, *our work …*

In this *paper / study / review* we have …

This paper has *investigated / explained / given an account of …*

Our research / This paper *has* highlighted / stressed / underlined *the importance of …*

We have managed to do / succeeded in doing / been able to do / found a way to do *X.*

We have found an innovative / a new / a novel / a cutting-edge *solution for …*

We have devised a methodology / procedure / strategy *which …*

We have confirmed / provided further evidence / demonstrated *that …*

The strength / strong point / value / impact / benefit / usefulness / significance / importance *of our* work / study / contribution *lies in …*

The results / findings *of this study* indicate / support the idea / suggest *that …*

In general, / Taken together, *these results* suggest / would seem to suggest *that …*

These findings add to a growing body of literature on / substantially to our understanding of *X.*

30 HIGHLIGHTING LIMITATIONS (SEE ALSO 28)

Finally, a number of potential limitations / weaknesses / shortfalls / shortcomings / weak points *need to be considered. First, …*

Our work clearly has some limitations. Nevertheless / Despite this *we believe our work could be* the basis / a framework / a starting point / a springboard for

Despite the fact that there are / In spite of the fact that / Although *there are limitations due to Y, we …*

The most important limitation lies in / is due to / is a result of *the fact that …*

The current study was limited by / unable to / not specifically designed to…

We only investigated / examined X. Therefore / Consequently …

The project / analysis / testing / sampling *was limited in several ways. First, …*

The findings might not be *transferable to / generalized to / representative of …*

The picture / situation *is thus still incomplete.*

8.5   Useful phrases (cont.)

31 APPLICATIONS AND IMPLICATIONS OF YOUR WORK

These observations have several / three main / many implications *for research into* …

The present findings might help to solve / have important implications for solving / suggest several courses of action *in order to solve this problem.*

Our method / technique / approach / procedure *could be applied to* …

One possible / potential / promising *application of our technique would be* …

This approach has the potential / requirements / characteristics / features *to* …

Our data suggest that X could be used / exploited / taken advantage of / made use of *in order to* …

We believe / are confident *that our results may improve knowledge about* …

We hope that our research will be helpful / useful / beneficial / constructive / valuable *in solving the difficulty of* … At the same time / In addition / Further / Furthermore *we believe that* ….

Our research suggests that *policy makers should / it is important for policy makers to* encourage stakeholders to …

The findings of my research have serious / considerable / important *managerial implications.*

32 FUTURE WORK

We are currently / now / in the process *of investigating* …

Research into solving this problem is already underway / in progress.

To further our research we plan / are planning / intend *to* …

Future work will concentrate on / focus on / explore / investigate / look into …

Further studies, which take X into account, will need to be undertaken / performed.

These findings suggest the following directions / opportunities *for future research:* ….

An important issue / matter / question / problem *to resolve for future studies is* …

We hope that further tests will prove our theory / confirm our findings.

Our results are encouraging / promising *and should be validated by a larger sample size.*

8.5 Useful phrases (cont.)

33 ACKNOWLEDGEMENTS

This work was carried out / performed *within the framework of an EU project and was partly sponsored by ...*

This research was made possible by / benefited from *a grant from ...*

Support was given by X, who funded the work in all its / its initial *stages.*

We thank / would like to thank *the following people for their support, without whose help this work would never have been possible:*

We gratefully acknowledge the help provided by Dr. X / constructive comments of the anonymous referees.

We are indebted / particularly grateful *to Dr. Alvarez for ...*

We thank / are grateful to / gratefully acknowledge *Dr. Y for her* help / valuable suggestions and discussions.

Thanks are also due to / The authors wish to thank *Prof. X, who gave us much valuable advice in the early stages of this work.*

Dr. Y collaborated with / worked alongside *our staff during this research project.*

We also thank Prof. Lim for her ongoing collaboration with our department / technical assistance in all our experimental work.

8.6 Exercises

1) Write one or two sentences maximum for each heading below.

Your most important findings, pointing out how these advance your field from the present state of knowledge.

_____

_____

The importance and significance of those findings in terms of their implications and impact, along with possible applications to other areas.

_____

_____

The limitations of your study and suggestions of how these limitations could be resolved in a future work by you and your research group.

_____

_____

Recommendations for future work (either for your research group, the community, policy makers etc).

_____

_____

2) Look at the beginnings of sentences below. Decide which ones you could use in your Conclusions. Complete the sentences.

1. We have described / presented _____

2. We have / In this paper it has been shown that _____

3. _____ has been described.

4. Our key findings were _____

5. Our findings highlight _____

6. Unfortunately, _____

7. Although _____

8. Despite this / Nevertheless, _____

9. Our findings could be applied / exploited _____

8.6 Exercises (cont.)

10. We suggest / recommend that _____

11. Further studies are needed to _____

12. Future work will involve _____

3) Using the sentences you have created in Exercises 1 and 2, write a Conclusions section on the topic of your research. You can invent whatever information you want, but make sure you follow the structure and tenses suggested in 7.3. You can use a personal or an impersonal style (see 2.6 and 9.6) or a mix of the two. You can also adapt the useful phrases shown in 8.5.

English for Academic Research: Writing Exercises

    How to be concise: 5.31

    Discussing limitations: 9.5–9.9

    Applications and future work: 9.16

    Structure: 10.12, 10.13

English for Academic Research: Grammar Exercises

    Tenses: Chapter 24

English for Academic Research: Vocabulary Exercises

    Useful phrases: 8.9–8.13

100 Typical Mistakes

    Chapter 4

English for Writing Research Papers

    Discussing limitations: Chapter 9

    Writing the Conclusions: Chapter 19

To practise writing the **Acknowledgements** see:

English for Academic Research: Writing Exercises

    10.14 and 10.15

English for Academic Research: Vocabulary Exercises

    Typical phrases: 8.14

Chapter 9
Abstracts Part 1

9.1 What is an Abstract?

1. What is an Abstract? a) a summary of the Introduction, Methods and Results b) a summary of the entire paper

2. How important is an Abstract? a) it is one of the most important aspects of a paper b) it is the most important aspect

3. How many paragraphs should an Abstract have? a) one b) several

4. What percentage of an Abstract should be devoted to talking about background information? a) 10–20% b) 20–35% c) 35–50%

5. How long should an Abstract be? a) 100–150 words b) 150–250 words c) 250–300 words

6. In what phase of writing a paper should you write your Abstract? a) first b) last c) first and last

7. What is the aim of an Abstract?

1. b – entire paper, but probably no mention of future work (see 8.3).

2. a – the title of the paper is probably more important, but the Abstract is more important than all the other sections of a paper.

3. depends on the journal. Medical journals generally request Abstracts with multiple paragraphs, known as structured abstracts (see 9.4). Humanities journals and other traditional/conservative science journals prefer single paragraphs.

4. a – there are no 'rules' on this, but background information is best given in the Introduction

5. depends on the journal, or conference (i.e. when you are submitting an abstract to a conference in the hope that you can do a presentation or poster)

© The Author(s), under exclusive license to Springer Nature Switzerland AG 2022
A. Wallwork, *Writing an Academic Paper in English*, English for Academic Research, https://doi.org/10.1007/978-3-030-95615-8_9

9.1   What is an Abstract? (cont.)

6. c – if you write it in the first phase (i.e. when you first start drafting the paper), it gives you an idea of how you need to structure the paper and what the most important elements and implications of your findings are. But you should then rewrite it when you have completed all the other sections.

7. essentially to encourage the reader to read the rest of the paper.

9.2   What information does an Abstract contain?

Imagine you are at a job interview at a research institute (see also 8.1). The inter-viewer says: *Tell me about yourself.* What would you say? Where would you start? How would you continue?

1. The professor or interviewer can probably imagine what you did in the first three quarters of your life, so you would probably begin with your first degree.

2. You then explain how this first degree influenced (or did not influence) your choice of topic in your Master's or PhD.

3. You recount the aim of your Master's / PhD studies.

4. You talk about what you did during your Master's / PhD, and what methodology you followed to achieve your initial aim.

5. You then tell the interviewer what you achieved during your Master's / PhD and why you believe these results to be important.

6. Finally, the interviewer might be interested to know what you plan to do next (e.g. the next step in your personal research agenda).

An Abstract follows a similar structure to points 1–6 above.

1. Brief background information.

2. Use background info to justify your choice of research topic.

3. State the aim of research.

4. Say what methods you used to achieve your initial aim.

5. Specify your results and why you believe these results to be important.

6. Finally, outline how your research area might develop in the future.

Note: Not all abstracts cover all six points, but certainly 3–5

9.2 What information does an Abstract contain? (cont.)

If you want to practise writing an Abstract, but in a non-academic context, then try the following exercise.

What is your favorite?

- a) book (fiction or non-fiction)
- b) movie
- c) music album or song

For either a, b, or c, answer as many of the following questions as you can:

1. What is the background? e.g. the historical / social / political / artistic context.

2. Why was the book written, movie made, album composed? What do you think was the aim of the writer, director, musician?

3. What method was used in the creative process? How different, if at all, was it from previous works?

4. What was the result? i.e. the level of success.

5. What were the implications? e.g. how did this work affect works that came after it, or what impact did it have on the social / political / artistic scenario?

Note: If the above task is too difficult, summarize the plot of a book or movie in 150 words. Be as concise as possible and use the most specific (technical) words you can. Use formal English.

9.3 What is the difference between an Abstract and an Introduction?

An Abstract summarizes ALL the sections of your paper, like a mini paper. It is NOT an introduction (see Chapter 2).

An Abstract answers these key questions:

1. Why did I perform this study?

2. What did I do, and how?

3. What were my results? What was new compared to previous research?

4. What are the implications (and limitations) of my findings? What are my conclusions and/or recommendations?

The structure, number of words, and style (*we investigated* vs *it was investigated*) depend on the journal or conference. Read the instructions to authors (1.5) in your chosen journal before you begin writing.

Based on your Abstract, i) editors may decide whether or not to send your paper for review; ii) readers will decide whether to read the rest of the paper.

Choose one or more of the four questions above. Write 40–50 words.

Alternatively:

Go on LinkedIn and find the profile of someone who works in a similar field to you. Look at your chosen person's *About* section (i.e. a summary of their experience). Write a similar one for yourself.

Some people write their *About* section with minimum use of verbs and personal pronouns. They do this to make their *About* section as concise as possible to make it quick for readers to get an immediate idea of their experience. For the purposes of this exercise, use verbs and pronouns, i.e. write it as if it were a normal text.

9.4   What is a Structured Abstract?

Many journals require a single paragraph.

Other journals require a 'structured abstract' i.e. short paragraphs with headings.

The headings in a structured abstract can vary (check with your journal).:

1. Background / Context / Purpose – Methods – Results / Findings – Conclusions

2. Context – Aim / Objective – Design – Setting – Patients (or Participants) – Interventions / Treatment – Main Outcome Measure(s) – Results – Conclusions

3. Context – Objective – Data Sources – Study Selection – Data Extraction – Results – Conclusions

4. Question – Location – Methods – Results – Conclusions

5. Purpose – Design / Methodology / Approach – Findings – Practical implications – Originality / Value – Keywords – Paper type

Look at the five sets of headings for a structured abstract listed above.

Which of the five sets would be most suitable for your paper? If no set is suitable, create your own headings.

Write 40–50 words for one of the headings in your chosen set. Do not choose a heading that covers the same ground as in the exercise in 9.3.

A structured abstract is much clearer to read. It is also easier for you to write. You will automatically include all the information that the editor, reviewers and your future readers require.

If your journal requires a single paragraph, write it like a structured paragraph but remove the headings.

9.4 What is a Structured Abstract? (cont.)

Below is an example of a Structured Abstract. Note: the numbers (1–5) in the Abstract below would not appear in a journal, they are just for the purposes of this book.

1 Background Queue jumping is considered to be a selfish behavior because it promotes the interest of the queue jumper to the detriment of the others in the queue. Previous research has shown that one in seven people jump queues, and that males tend to jump queues more than females.

2 Objective This paper investigates whether three other behaviors may be more indicative of selfish behavior than queue jumping: i) playing loud music in public places (e.g. on beaches), ii) double parking, and iii) dropping litter. We also related the level of selfishness to whether someone breaks their egg at the big end (big-enders: BEs) or small end (small-enders: SEs).

3 Methods CCTV cameras were located in Canada in public parks and outside fast-food restaurants and cinemas. A total of 10,000 hours of video recordings were processed using SelfiGit v. 16.1 (MacroHard Inc, US) to identify the number of occurrences of the selfish behaviors.

4 Results Of the 765,854 people videoed, approximately two thirds demonstrated no selfish behaviors. The majority of these were small-enders. Of the remaining one third, who were predominantly big-enders, 70% were caught on camera dropping litter; 15% double parking, 10% playing loud music, but only 5% queue jumping. An equal number of men and women were shown to drop litter, but in the three other cases there were four times as many men than women adopting the selfish behaviors.

5 Discussion and Conclusions The results of this study show that selfish behavior is very common in many aspects of daily life and is perpetrated more often by BEs than SEs. It impacts not only on other people but also on the environment. Future work will investigate the link between selfishness, egg-breaking habits, and climate change.

Write a structured abstract for your own research. If you don't have any results yet, imagine what they might be.

134

9.5 My journal requires a single paragraph Abstract. How should I structure it?

The decision to use one or multiple paragraphs does NOT depend on you. To understand how many paragraphs you should use and the total word count (i.e. the maximum number of words you can use), look at papers that have already been published by your journal. In any case, most journal websites have a section called 'Instructions to Authors' (1.5) where they state how a paper should be written.

*****

Below is the same abstract as in 9.4, but this time written as one paragraph. Note how it follows exactly the same structure (1–5). However, in some places I have changed the style from impersonal to personal (i.e. using we/our) – can you see where?

(1) Queue jumping is considered to be a selfish behavior because it promotes the interest of the queue jumper to the detriment of the others in the queue. Previous research has shown that one in seven people jump queues, and that males tend to jump queues more than females. **(2)** We investigated whether three other behaviors may be more indicative of selfish behavior than queue jumping: i) playing loud music in public places (e.g. on beaches), ii) double parking, and iii) dropping litter. We also related the level of selfishness to whether someone breaks their egg at the big end (big-enders: BEs) or small end (small-enders: SEs). **(3)** CCTV cameras were located in parks, in the street, outside cinemas and on public beaches. We analysed a total of 10,000 hours of video recordings, which were processed using SelfiGit v. 16.1 (MacroHard Inc, US) to identify the number of occurrences of the selfish behaviors. **(4)** Of the 765,854 people videoed, approximately two thirds demonstrated no selfish behaviors. Of the remaining one third, 70% were caught on camera dropping litter; 15% double parking, 10% playing loud music, but only 5% queue jumping. An equal number of men and women were shown to drop litter, but in the three other cases there were four times as many men than women adopting the selfish behaviors. **(5)** Our results show that selfish behavior is very common in many aspects of daily life and is perpetrated more often by BEs than SEs. It impacts not only on other people but also on the environment. We now plan to investigate the link between selfishness, egg-breaking habits, and climate change.

(2) We investigated … (3) We analysed … (5) Our results … We now plan …

The use of a personal vs impersonal style is discussed in 9.6.

9.6 Should I use a personal style (e.g. *we found*) or an impersonal style (e.g. *it was found*)?

An impersonal style can be:

- in the active form, but NOT using a personal pronoun (*we, I*). This paper **investigates** ...
- in the passive form (*to be* + past participle): Smokers **were found** ...

A personal style uses the active form: **We found** that ...

Look at the three pairs of sentences below.

The first sentence (a) in each pair is written in an impersonal style: the person who did the action is not mentioned, although in most cases it will be the authors of the paper.

The second sentence in each pair (b) is written in a personal style using *we*.

For each pair, decide which you think is better a or b, or if there is no difference.

1a This paper **investigates** the percentage of queue jumpers that leave litter on a beach.

1b **We investigated** the percentage of queue jumpers that leave litter on a beach.

2a CCTV cameras **were positioned** outside bars.

2b **We positioned** CCTV cameras outside bars.

3a Big-enders **were found** to be much more likely to behave selfishly.

3b **We found** that big-enders are much more likely to behave selfishly.

Both 1a and 1b are commonly used, though 1b is shorter and more direct.

2a and 2b refer to your methods (see Chapter 4 Methods) – usually the reader can immediately that you are talking about your methods, so the passive form (2a) tends to be preferred.

3a may be ambiguous – did you get this result or someone else? This tends to cause confusion in the Discussion (see 7.4). If there could be any ambiguity, prefer 3b.

9.6 Should I use a personal style (e.g. *we found*) or an impersonal style (e.g. *it was found*)? (cont.)

Consult the 'Instructions to Authors' (1.5) on the website of your journal to understand if you should use an impersonal or personal style. If the journal doesn't specify, look at examples of papers published by the journal to see which style is typically used.

A mix of a personal and impersonal style is perfectly acceptable if the journal does not prohibit personal forms.

Look at the abstract you wrote in 9.4. Underline all the verbs and decide which ones it would be appropriate to use *we*. Are there any cases where you could replace *the* with *our*?

9.7 What tenses are typically used in an abstract?

The tenses shown below appear in the order that they would normally used in an abstract. However, the present perfect is not always required in an abstract.

PRESENT SIMPLE what is already known – facts <u>not</u> found by you, but by others in the scientific community.

> It **is well known** that queue jumping **is** a sign of selfish behavior.

> Queue jumping **is considered** to be a selfish behavior because it **causes** longer waits for others in the queue.

PRESENT PERFECT to refer to previous work or to refer to a situation that began in the past continues into the present.

> Although several papers **have been written** on the topic of selfish behavior, to date no studies **have analysed** the importance of ...

SIMPLE PRESENT or SIMPLE PAST to state the aim of your paper.

> This paper **investigates** the percentage of queue jumpers that leave litter on a beach.

> **We investigated** the possible correlation between queue jumping and leaving litter on a beach.

SIMPLE PAST what <u>you</u> did in your research, e.g. to describe your methods.

> CCTV cameras **were located** outside bars.

> **We positioned** CCTV cameras outside bars.

SIMPLE PAST your results.

> People who break an egg at the big end **were found** to be much more likely to behave selfishly.

> **We found** that people who break an egg at the big end have a greater probability of exhibiting selfish behavior.

9.7 What tenses are typically used in an abstract? (cont.)

SIMPLE PRESENT in the concluding sentences: implications of your findings

> Several selfish behaviors **are often shown** by big-enders. Selfish behavior **benefits** the individual in terms of ...

> Big-enders **often behave** selfishly in various areas of their life. Individuals **tend** to behave selfishly in order to ...

WILL or SIMPLE PRESENT IN the concluding sentences: what you plan to do next.

> Future work **will investigate** the link between egg-breaking habits and climate change.

> In a future study, we **plan** to examine the connection between climate change and ....

Note: In some disciplines the Abstract may be written entirely in the SIMPLE PRESENT, particularly in physics, mathematics and engineering. Below is an example – I have replaced the key words with x, y and z.

> An x **is proposed** for the determination of y. Numerical procedures **are provided** for z. An experimental example **is shown** on xyz. A parametric analysis **is then presented** to evaluate the size effects on x.

Find two or three abstracts on your topic of research written by native English-speaking authors. Underline all the verbs. For each verb: i) identify the tense; ii) analyse if it matches the guidelines given above. For those tenses that do not match the guidelines, decide if there is a logical reason.

Exercises

English for Academic Research: Writing Exercises

> Structure: 10.1

English for Academic Research: Grammar Exercises

> Tenses: Chapter 19

Chapter 10
Abstracts Part 2 and Titles

10.1 Typical mistakes made in Abstracts

✎

The abstract below is typical of many abstracts, but it is NOT written well. Which of the following do you find difficult to understand?

a) what the researchers were trying to do

b) what method they used

c) what the result was

d) what the implications were

Elements of selfish behavior have been studied regarding three types of selfish acts characteristic of citizens in the USA. Investigations into selfish behavior are essential to understand why for example, people do not differentiate their trash, or insist on driving large high-fuel consumption cars. In the selfish acts examined the behavior can be described by a Hyperego equation highlighting the relationship between the selfish act and the consequences on the rest of the population. This selfish behavior phenomenon can be attributed to the lack of empathetic bonds of a sufficient strength between the perpetrator of the selfish act and members of his / her family and friendship network. The results obtained also by means of a distribution coefficient, show a different behavior of the egoist vs the non-egoist, which may be ascribable to whether they break their egg at the big or small end, respectively. In the egoists, dropping litter was the main characteristic. Also queue jumping plays a fundamental role in highlighting the level of selfishness of a subject. The study of selfish behavior in the USA is currently of considerable interest due to the growing concerns deriving from acts of selfishness having a detrimental health effect (including mortality) on other members of the population, through non-green behaviors and non community-oriented behaviors during pandemics. The data obtained could contribute to drafting public health regulations that are currently lacking for this reality.

© The Author(s), under exclusive license to Springer Nature
Switzerland AG 2022
A. Wallwork, *Writing an Academic Paper in English*, English for Academic
Research, https://doi.org/10.1007/978-3-030-95615-8_10

10.1 Typical mistakes made in Abstracts (cont.)

a) It is reasonably clear what the research area is – selfish behavior. But the authors have not stated their aims. Does *have been investigated* refer to what the authors' did or what others have done?

b) It seems that the authors of <u>this</u> paper used a *Hyperego equation* and a *distribution coefficient*. However this is not stated explicitly. *The behavior can be described by a Hyperego equation* – can be described by <u>who</u>? Do the <u>authors</u> describe this in their paper, or is this a general approach? *The results obtained also by means of a distribution coefficient* – did the authors use the *distribution coefficient* or are they referring to what others have done? It is not clear

c) In the text, various results are mentioned, but it is not 100% clear that these are the authors' results. Instead, if they had written *we found* that, it would be clear.

d) The implications are clear.

The main problem is that is not immediately clear for the reader which sentences relate to background information and which ones refer to the authors' work.

10.2   Improving / Editing your Abstract

Look at how an editor has improved the abstract given in 10.1. Which of the following has the editor done?

1) Used the personal pronoun (*we*) to make it clear what actions were carried out by the authors.

2) Used the simple past (and not the present perfect or present simple) to indicate what the authors did.

3) Divided up long sentences.

4) Used synonyms to avoid repeating the same word.

5) Deleted unnecessary words and reduce the length of phrases containing non-key words.

(1) We studied three types of selfish acts that are characteristic of citizens in the USA. Investigations into selfish behavior are essential to understand why for example, people do not differentiate their trash, or insist on driving large high-fuel consumption cars. **(2)** We used a Hyperego equation to describe the selfish acts. **(3)** The equation highlighted the relationship between the selfish act and the consequences on the rest of the population. **(4)** We believe that this selfish behavior **(5)** is due to the lack of **(6)** strong empathetic bonds between **(7)** perpetrators of selfish acts and members of their family and friendship network. **(8)** We also used a distribution coefficient, which revealed that **(9)** egoists behave differently from non-egoists. **(10)** This different behavior may be related to whether they break their egg at the big or small end, respectively. In the egoists, dropping litter and queue jumping are key to highlighting the level of selfishness. **(11)** Studying selfish behavior in the West is important **(12)** since selfishness appears to have a detrimental health effect (including mortality) on other members of the population, through non-green behaviors and non community-oriented behaviors during pandemics. **(13)** We believe that our data obtained could contribute to drafting new public health regulations

The editor has implemented 1, 2, 3 and 5, but not 4 (synonym for key words tend to confuse rather than help readers. Readers cannot know if author is always referring to the same thing, or different things).

10.2   Improving / Editing your Abstract (cont.)

Now look at the numbers in bold in the edited text. For each number (or at least for the first six), discuss what the editor has done and why.

1) Clarifies who did the *investigation*.

2) Clarifies who used the *equation*.

3) Divides up long sentence. This entails repeating the subject (*equation*).

4) Clarifies that this is just the authors' opinion which is not necessarily reflected in the literature.

5) More concise – deletes non key words.

6) Same as 5.

7) The editor has made *perpetrator* plural (*perpetrators*). This avoids having to use *his/her*.

8) Clarifies who used the *distribution coefficient*.

9) Uses a verb (*behave*) rather than a noun (*behavior*). Using verbs creates variety, is more dynamic, and reduces the number of words that need to be used.

10) Same as 3.

11) Same as 9.

12) Same as 5.

13) Writing *we believe* makes their assertion less strong.

10.3 Why improving / editing your Abstract is so important

Look at the original version and edited version of the first part of the Abstract that you read in 10.1 and 10.2. Analyse why the edited version is more likely to be accepted for publication and more likely to be read by potential readers.

ORIGINAL VERSION	EDITED VERSION
Elements of selfish behavior have been studied regarding three types of selfish acts characteristic of citizens in the West. Investigations into selfish behavior are essential to understand why for example, people do not differentiate their trash, or insist on driving large high-fuel consumption cars. In the selfish acts examined the behavior can be described by a Hyperego equation highlighting the relationship between the selfish act and the consequences on the rest of the population. This selfish behavior phenomenon can be attributed to the lack of empathetic bonds of a sufficient strength between the perpetrator of the selfish act and members of his / her family and friendship network.	We studied three types of selfish acts that are characteristic of citizens in the West. Investigations into selfish behavior are essential to understand why for example, people do not differentiate their trash, or insist on driving large high-fuel consumption cars. We used a Hyperego equation to describe the selfish acts. The equation highlighted the relationship between the selfish act and the consequences on the rest of the population. We believe that this selfish behavior is due to the lack of strong empathetic bonds between perpetrators of selfish acts and members of their family and friendship network.

Here are three key reasons why the edited version is so much more effective than the original version.

1. It is 12 words shorter: 96 words vs 108 words. This means that it is quicker to read, even though the information contained is exactly the same. Abstracts usually have a limit on the number of words you can use. Consequently, learning how to be more concise and how to reduce redundancy are fundamental – not just in the Abstract but in the rest of the paper too.

10.3 Why improving / editing your Abstract is so important (cont.)

2. There is a clear differentiation between what the authors did (*we*) and what is already known. If your journal prohibits the use of *we*, then you MUST find other ways to make it 100% clear when you are talking about what you did. You could replace *We studied* in the first line with *This paper studies*. Instead of writing *We used a Hyperego equation*, you can say: *A Hyperego equation was used*. The reader is likely to understand that this was your method as you have used the past tense (*was used* rather than *has been used*). Generally, the past tense is used to refer to your own work. But it is not 100% immediately clear. *We believe that this selfish behavior is due to* could be rewritten as *This selfish behavior is likely due to* ... but again it would still not be 100% clear that this is your opinion.

3. The sentences are shorter in the edited version. This makes them easier to read and understand for the editor, reviewers and readers (as well as your co-authors).

10.4 Writing a Title

1. Do you always understand the titles of other people's papers? What are the typical faults?

2. How difficult do you find it to write a title?

3. How quickly do you tend to write your title? a) 2–3 minutes b) 20–30 minutes c) more than 30 minutes

4. At what point in your paper writing schedule do you write the title?

5. What do you need to think about before writing your title?

The best moment to write a title is when you have the final version of your abstract and you have finished the rest of the manuscript. However, it is also a good idea to write a provisional title <u>before</u> you start writing. Writing a title forces you to think about the following:

- What have I found that will attract attention?

- What is new, different and interesting about my findings?

- What are the 3–5 key words that highlight what makes my research and my findings unique?

On the basis of your answers you should be able to formulate a title. This title should have a definite and concise indication of what is written in the paper itself. In my opinion an ideal title does not merely give an indication of the topic, but also gives your main result.

Every word in your title is important. So the key is to devise a title that:

- is not more than one and half lines long. But don't be too concise – it is important that you readers can understand it

- will immediately make sense to the referee and will attract potential readers

- will easily be found by a search engine or indexing system

Do not write your title at the last minute. Draft it, rewrite it trying to put key words at the beginning, and eliminate redundant words (but don't be too concise). Basically, spend time on your title. It is the most important element in your paper. If your readers don't understand the title or don't find it stimulating, they won't read your paper.

10.5   Typical problems with Titles

Decide which of the following contain good advice (GA), and which contain bad or misleading advice (BA).

1. Try to put your key words as near as possible to the beginning of the title.

2. Avoid beginning with phrase such as: *A study of ... An investigation into ... An innovative method for ...*

3. Putting a series of adjectives and nouns in sequence will make the title more concise and is better style, e.g. *A novel automatic title writing generator for international journal academic paper publishing*

4. Avoid using a lot of prepositions.

5. Avoid using words such as *new*, *novel* and *innovative*.

6. A title must be grammatically correct – it is not a text message.

7. Check the spelling.

8. Check with the Instructions for Authors of your journal to see if they prefer specific types of title, and compare your title with titles of other papers in your chosen journal.

1, 2) GA. None of these phrases in 2) contain key words and they will not be used in searches either by individual users or by search engines. Instead, try to shift key words to the beginning as they are more likely to be indexed by search engines.

3, 4) BA. Putting a sequence of nouns and adjectives tends to make a title incomprehensible. Instead you need to put adjectives directly before the noun they require, and break up sequences of nouns by using prepositions and verbs. Repeating the same preposition two or even three times is not a problem. In the following title it is difficult to understand how the various words relate to each other

> *A novel automatic title writing generator for international journal academic paper publishing*

It would be better to write:

> *An automatic generator for writing the titles of papers intended for publication in international journals*

10.5   Typical problems with Titles (cont.)

5) BA. By default your paper should be providing new information. In fact, some journals even prohibit the use of *new*, *novel* and *innovative* in titles.

6) GA. You must include articles (*the, a/an*) where necessary: see Chapter 1 in the companion volume *Grammar, Usage and Strategies*. It also helps if you use a verb (e.g. *intended* in the title above) as verbs tend to highlight relationships between key words.

7) GA. Titles often contain very specific technical words or names of people (*Alzheimer's*). Such words may not be contained in the dictionary of your writing program.

8) GA.

Write a title for a paper that describes the research you have done so far.

- Make sure, if possible, that it summarizes as much as possible the aim (and possibly the result) of your research. Ensure that the key words are near the beginning of the title.

- Show it (either in English or in your language) to a member of the family – if they can't understand it at all, then it probably needs modifying.

- Then show it to a colleague – see if you colleague can improve it to make the key aim and result stand out.

10.6 Do's and Don'ts of writing the Abstract

Spend time a lot of time on your Abstract. It needs to be as clear as possible. If you force your readers to make a lot of a mental effort to understand your abstract, they may decide not to read the rest of the paper. Instead, to encourage your readers to continue reading, in your Abstract:

DO have a clear structure: i) current situation, ii) what you did, iii) why you did it, iv) what you found, v) what your findings mean. Points i, ii and iii may be in a different order.

DON'T automatically opt for an impersonal style (i.e. no personal pronouns, and predominantly passive forms). If your journal allows, use *we*. This helps the reader to differentiate between what YOU did and what OTHERS have done.

DO be careful of your use of tenses. Generally, use the PRESENT SIMPLE to describe the current situation and what is known already. Use the PAST SIMPLE to describe what you did in your study.

DO break up a long sentence into two shorter sentences.

DO use the most specific words possible.

DO repeat key words instead of finding synonyms.

DON'T exceed the word count (i.e. the maximum number of words permitted by your journal).

10.7 Useful phrases

34 IMPORTANCE OF YOUR TOPIC

X is the main / leading / primary / major *cause of ...*

Xs are attracting considerable / increasing / widespread *interest due to ...*

X has many uses / roles / applications *in the field of ...*

35 GAP IN KNOWLEDGE AND POSSIBLE LIMITATIONS

Few researchers have addressed the problem / issue / question *of ...*

Previous work has only focused on / been limited to / failed to address ...

A basic / common / fundamental / crucial / major *issue of ...*

A major defect / difficulty / drawback / disadvantage / flaw *of X is ...*

Despite this interest, no one to the best of our knowledge / as far as we know *has studied ...*

36 AIM OF YOUR PAPER AND ITS CONTRIBUTION

In this report / paper / review / study *we ...*

This paper outlines / proposes / describes / presents *a new approach to ...*

X is presented / described / analyzed / computed / investigated / examined / introduced / discussed *in order to ...*

The aim of our work / research / study / analysis *was to* further / extend / widen / broaden *current knowledge of ...*

The aim of this study is to study / evaluate / validate / determine / examine / analyze / calculate / estimate / formulate ...

We describe / present / consider / analyze *a* novel / simple / radical / interesting *solution for ...*

37 PURPOSE OF TESTING AND METHODS USED

In order to identify / understand / investigate / study / analyze *X ...*

To enable / allow *us to ..., we ...*

To see / determine / check / verify / determine *whether ...*

X was done / We did X *in order to ...*

38 WHAT YOU FOUND

These tests revealed / showed / highlighted *that ...*

Strong / Some / No evidence *of X was found ...*

10.7 Useful phrases (cont.)

There was a significant positive / no *correlation between* …

On average / Generally speaking / Broadly speaking, *we found values for X of* …

Further analysis / analyses / tests / examinations / replications *showed that* …

39 BENEFITS OF YOUR APPROACH, METHOD, EQUIPMENT ETC

This method represents a viable / valuable / useful / groundbreaking / innovative *alternative to* …

This approach has several / many *interesting* features / characteristics.

Our procedure is a clear improvement / advance *on current methods.*

For phrases regarding the possible implications and applications of your research see Useful Phrases 31.

10.8 Exercises

1) Write one or two sentences maximum for each heading below.

Background to your research.

_____

A specific difficulty related to the current situation in your research area.

_____

The aim of your study.

_____

Your method.

_____

Your results.

_____

What your results mean.

_____

2) Fill in the spaces. Add additional sentences as required.

1. We investigated _____

2. This topic requires investigation because _____

3. Our aim was to _____

4. We used _____

5. We found that _____

6. Our results would seem to indicate that _____

3) Using the sentences you have created in Exercises 1 and 2, write an abstract on the topic of your research. You can invent whatever information you want, but make sure you follow the structure and tenses suggested in this chapter. Use an impersonal style (9.6) – this means that you will have to transform the sentences in Exercise 2 from a personal to an impersonal style. You can also adapt phrases from 10.6.

10.8 Exercises (cont.)

English for Academic Research: Writing Exercises

Being concise in Abstracts: 5.25

Structure in Abstracts: 10.1

Reducing the word count in Titles: 5.4

English for Academic Research: Grammar Exercises

Grammar in Titles: Chapter 18

English for Academic Research: Vocabulary Exercises

Useful phrases in Abstracts: 8.1–8.3

100 Typical Mistakes

Chapter 1 Titles and Abstracts

English for Writing Research Papers

Writing a Title: Chapter 12

Writing an Abstract: Chapter 13

Chapter 11
How to write and structure a paper: a very brief summary

11.1 Writing and communication skills

This chapter uses tables to summarize

- the aim of each section

- how to organize each section in a logical reader-friendly way

- the tenses you will typically need

- whether you can / should use a personal form (*we found*) rather than an impersonal and possibly ambiguous form (*it was found*)

- key points to remember when writing a particular section

BUT … Knowing what to write and how to organize it is really only half the problem. A key issue is **ensuring that your paper is readable.**

So you need to know HOW to write it – how to write clearly, concisely and unambiguously.

These points are detailed in the companion volume *Grammar, Usage and Strategies*. Below are the chapter titles. The chapters that will help you the most to improve your writing style and the readability of your paper are highlighted in bold.

1. Articles and nouns

2. Abbreviations, Acronyms, False friends, Spelling

3. Can, may, could, might

4. **Clarity and Empathy**

5. Comparisons, Dates, Measurements, Numbers

6. CVs / Resumes

7. Emails

8. **Link words**

9. **Paragraphs, Sentence length, Paraphrasing**

A. Wallwork, *Writing an Academic Paper in English*, English for Academic Research, https://doi.org/10.1007/978-3-030-95615-8_11

11.1   Writing and communication skills (cont.)

10. Prepositions and Adverbs

11. Present and Past Tenses

12. Punctuation, Genitive

13. Verbs

14. Word order

If your level of English is quite advanced, then you can find much more detailed information on writing style in the *English for Academic Research* series: *English for Writing Research Papers.* Below are the chapter titles. Again, the chapters that will help you the most to improve your writing style and the readability of your paper are highlighted in bold.

PART 1 WRITING SKILLS

1. Planning and Preparation
2. **Structuring a sentence: word order**
3. **Structuring paragraphs**
4. **Breaking up long sentences**
5. **Being concise and removing redundancy**
6. **Avoiding ambiguity, repetition, and vague language**
7. **Clarifying who did what**
8. **Highlighting your findings**
9. Discussing your limitations
10. Hedging and criticising
11. Plagiarism and paraphrasing

PART 2 SECTIONS OF A PAPER

12. Titles
13. Abstracts
14. Introduction
15. Review of the Literature
16. Methods
17. Results
18. Discussion
19. Conclusions
20. The Final Check

Another key aspect of writing a paper is getting it published! To get it published you need to know how to interact via email with editors and reviewers. Chapter 7 in the companion volume *Grammar, Usage and Strategies* will help you to **communicate better with the journal** and thus increase your chances of being published. For further details see *English for Academic Correspondence,* which is another volume in the *English for Academic Research* series. Key chapters are:

11.1 Writing and communication skills (cont.)

Finally, there are aspects to writing research papers that no books can teach you ... but colleagues and professors can! **Always ask for their feedback**. They understand your research so they should be able to tell you whether you have included everything and that everything makes sense. You need to make their task relatively easy. So instead of emailing someone an entire paper for their feedback, you can email them just one section. If the sections are very long, then you can just highlight the parts that you would like them to read.

To make their task easier (and more useful to you in terms of their answers), you can ask them specific questions:

Does the title give you a clear idea of the topic?

Does the article fit the aims and scope of the journal?

Does the abstract accurately describe the content?

Is the Introduction written grammatically and clearly?

Have I included all the steps in the methodology?

Are there any key results that I have not highlighted?

Are the conclusions borne out (supported) by the evidence and arguments?

You can find lots of similar questions by looking at the forms that reviewers are asked to fill in by editors. If you know some colleagues and professors who have done peer reviews of papers, then ask them for the questions that they had to answer.

11.2   Title

AIM	To attract readers to YOUR paper rather than another paper. To include key words that search engines will index.
STRUCTURE	Key words at the beginning. More general concepts at the end.
GRAMMAR	Prepositions are normally essential. Verbs help to make the title more immediately understandable. Articles (*the/a*) are not merely an optional – the title must be grammatically correct.
DON'T FORGET	If readers don't immediately understand the title, they won't read the paper.

11.3 Abstract

AIM	To encourage readers to read the rest of the paper.
STRUCTURE	Should summarize <u>all</u> the sections of the paper. Background info: 20% max. One paragraph or multiple paragraphs with headings – depends on the journal. **i)** Brief background information. **ii)** Use background info to justify your choice of research topic. **iii)** State the aim of research. **iv)** Say what methods you used to achieve your initial aim. **v)** Specify your results and why you believe these results to be important. **vi)** Outline how your research area might develop in the future (this info is not always included in an Abstract).
TENSES	PRESENT SIMPLE (what is already known; to explain importance of your work). PAST SIMPLE (what <u>you</u> did, found).
WE VS IMPERSONAL	A mix. But look at abstracts in your chosen journal to see the typical style.
DON'T FORGET	You only have a limited number of words. For maximum impact: i) Remove any words and phrases that are redundant. ii) Keep sentences short and simple. iii) Be concise.

11.4 Introduction

AIM	To give readers the minimum amount of info they need to be able to understand the context (state of the art) of your research and how your study addresses the key issues that still need resolving.
STRUCTURE	You need to cover some or all of the following, but not necessarily in this order: **i)** Definition of your topic. **ii)** State of art + problem to be resolved. **iii)** Your objectives. **iv)** Review of the literature (unless this is in a separate section). **v)** Problems revealed by review (gap to fill). **vi)** The aim of your paper in relation to points i) to v).
TENSES	PRESENT SIMPLE: general background, i.e. what is known already; to give structure of paper. PRESENT PERFECT: how the problem has been approached from the past until the present day. In the examples, the exact time when the actions were carried out is not given. PAST SIMPLE: what specific authors have done, what your aim was and what you did.
WE VS IMPERSONAL	Very important to differentiate what YOU did vs what OTHERS have done. So use *we* or *in our study*, unless it is 100% clear to the reader that you are now talking about your work and not someone else's.
DON'T FORGET	The Introduction is not a chronological list of all previous work. Just select the works that are relevant to your topic and always ensure you state how your work develops on or differs from the previous works. Introductions are typically full of redundant phrases: Be concise!

11.5 Review of the Literature

AIM	To give the context for your specific research and to enable readers to see how your paper extends the work of previous papers, or fills a gap (i.e. something that has not been the subject of research, but merits being studied).
STRUCTURE	A series of paragraphs where you repeat the following steps: **i)** Give current status. **ii)** Point out the achievements so far. **iii)** Tell the reader what you think are the current drawbacks / limitations, **iv)** Show how you work expands on ii) and solves iii). Repeat this structure for each of the groups of authors that you review.
TENSES, WE VS IMPERS., DON'T FORGET	See Introduction.

11.6   Methods

AIM	To enable your readers to replicate your experiments.
STRUCTURE	**i)** Quick definition / overview **ii)** Materials / samples used **iii)** Source of data **iv)** Method / procedure **v)** Validation
TENSES	PAST SIMPLE: what steps you followed. PRESENT SIMPLE: to describe known formulas, protocols, procedures, laws, tests (i.e. not things that you invented yourself).
WE VS IMPERSONAL	Impersonal (passive).
DON'T FORGET	Put the steps of your method in chronological order. Help the reader by using terms such as *first(ly), second(ly), finally*.

11.7 Results

AIM	i) To report the results without subjective interpretation (such interpretations are given in the Discussion). ii) To enable readers to 'see' and understand the results quickly and easily.
STRUCTURE	**i)** Restate aim of your research in one succinct sentence. **ii)** Very briefly remind readers about your methodology and why you chose it. **iii)** Refer to a figure or table, and highlight the key points. **iv)** Repeat step iii for all your tables and figures. **v)** Explain how you analysed your results. **vi)** 1–2 sentence summary of what your results mean. Most Results sections do not compare your key findings with previous work. But if you do make such comparisons, simply comment on the differences without stating the implications (instead, do this in the Discussion).
TENSES	PAST SIMPLE: to describe your results PRESENT SIMPLE: to refer to tables and figures and what they show
WE VS IMPERSONAL	Impersonal (passive). Use *we* and *our* if you are differentiating your results from another author's (although this is usually done in the Discussion)
DON'T FORGET	Mention all relevant info, including data that do not support your hypotheses. This is a summary of your results; you are NOT reporting them in full detail. If you need to give more details, consider putting them as supplementary material.

11.8 Discussion

AIM	To connect what you mentioned in your review of the literature (i.e. the gap you wanted to fill, the limitations of current studies) with your results. Help readers understand how your results fill the gap and overcome current limitations.
STRUCTURE	**i)** Re-state the aim of your research. **ii)** Briefly summarize your key results. **iii)** Compare <u>one</u> of the key results with others in literature, highlighting similarities and differences. **iv)** State the implications of the comparison you made in step iii). **v)** Repeat steps iii) and iv) for each of your key results. **vi)** Mention any limitations to your study. **vii)** Restate the importance of your work
TENSES	The Discussion uses more tenses than the other sections. Below are just the key tenses and verb forms. PRESENT SIMPLE: known facts (*smoking causes cancer*), what your findings appear to reveal (*PhD students study too much*), make recommendations and proposals (*we thus suggest / propose that*) PRESENT PERFECT: refer to your and other authors' results (*we / Smith found that x = y*) WOULD, MAY, MIGHT, COULD: to speculate on what might have caused your results or what they might mean (*this would seem to indicate that, this may have been caused by*).
WE VS IMPERSONAL	Very important to differentiate what YOU did vs what OTHERS have done. So use *we* or *in our study*, unless it is 100% clear to the reader that you are now talking about your work and not someone else's.
DON'T FORGET	Highlight your key findings (short sentences, new paragraphs), compare them with the literature, and explain why they are important. Readers must finish your paper with a clear idea of what the problem is, how you have contributed to resolving the problem, and what the implications are of your solution.

11.9 Conclusions

AIM	To answer these questions: What have we learned? What does this all mean? What are the implications? What will we / should we do next?
STRUCTURE	**i)** 1–2 sentences summarizing aim and main findings. **ii)** 1–2 sentences highlighting how your work has filled a gap or improved knowledge. **iii)** 3 or more sentences explaining the importance of your work and how it will impact on the scientific community, and possibly on society in general. **iv)** 1–3 sentences on what needs to be done in the future (either by you or the scientific community in general). If your journal recommends mentioning your limitations in the Conclusions (rather than the Discussion), then insert them between points ii and iii, NOT at the end. You want readers to feel positive at the end of your paper.
TENSES	The Conclusions contain a mix of the tenses used in all the other parts of the paper. In addition: PRESENT PERFECT: in the first sentence to describe what you have done in the paper e.g. *We have presented a new model for solving x ...*
WE VS IMPERSONAL	See Discussion.
DON'T FORGET	The Conclusions section is NOT a summary of the paper (the Abstract is the summary). The Conclusions <u>may</u> be the last section your readers read. Ensure they end your paper feeling positive about your work.

11.10   Acknowledgements

AIM	To thank those people who helped you in your research project, or who gave you materials, funded you etc.
STRUCTURE	A few sentences beginning like this: *We would like to thank ...* *Thanks are also due to ...* *Finally, we would like to thank ...*
WE VS IMPERSONAL	*We would like to thank / The authors would like to thank ...*

11.11 Formatting your paper for offline and online reading and editing

Look at the three formats (A, B, C) below. You don't need to read the text. Imagine you had to choose one of these formats to enable you to check and edit your paper. Obviously, if you were submitting a paper to a journal you would have to follow the journal's guidelines.

1. Which is easiest to read on your screen?

2. Which is easiest to edit directly on your screen?

3. Which is easiest to read and/or edit when printed?

11.11 Formatting your paper for offline and online reading and editing (cont.)

A

We investigated a series of selfish behaviors to understand whether they are more frequently shown by big-enders (BEs) and small-enders (SEs), and what the consequent implications are on community living. We also compared these behaviors with right-handers and left-handers, i.e. people with a propensity to use one hand rather than the other to break their eggs. Other authors have studied selfish behavior of BEs and SEs in relation to level of income (Dosh et al, 2020), level of education and critical thinking (Schule et al, 2019), intelligence quotient and cognitive dissonance (Iqbal & Mensa, 2025), musical taste (Hamonija, 2026), taste in movies (Flix & Odeon, 2027), and historical tyrants (Des Pott et al, 2028). However, in all cases the sample sizes were relatively small - education (501 subjects), IQ (145), music (88), movies (345), and tyrants (29). Our sample was approximately 10,000 people spread over three continents (N. America, Europe and Asia). In fact, to the best of our knowledge our sample is the largest ever used in a psycho-social study of endedness, where 'endedness' is defined as the tendency to break an egg at one end more frequently than the other end.

B

We investigated a series of selfish behaviors to understand whether they are more frequently shown by big-enders (BEs) and small-enders (SEs), and what the consequent implications are on community living. We also compared these behaviors with right-handers and left-handers, i.e. people with a propensity to use one hand rather than the other to break their eggs. Other authors have studied selfish behavior of BEs and SEs in relation to level of income (Dosh et al, 2020), level of education and critical thinking (Schule et al, 2019), intelligence quotient and cognitive dissonance (Iqbal & Mensa, 2025), musical taste (Hamonija, 2026), taste in movies (Flix & Odeon, 2027), and historical tyrants (Des Pott et al, 2028). However, in all cases the sample sizes were relatively small - education (501 subjects), IQ (145), music (88), movies (345), and tyrants (29).

C

We investigated a series of selfish behaviors to understand whether they are more frequently shown by big-enders (BEs) and small-enders (SEs), and what the consequent implications are on community living. We also compared these behaviors with right-handers and left-handers, i.e. people with a propensity to use one hand rather than the other to break their eggs. Other authors have studied selfish behavior of BEs and SEs in relation to level of income (Dosh et al, 2020), level of education and critical thinking (Schule et al, 2019), intelligence quotient and cognitive dissonance (Iqbal & Mensa, 2025), musical taste (Hamonija, 2026), taste in movies (Flix & Odeon, 2027), and historical tyrants (Des Pott et al, 2028). However, in all cases the sample sizes were relatively small - education (501 subjects), IQ (145), music (88), movies (345), and tyrants (29).

11.11   Formatting your paper for offline and online reading and editing (cont.)

How you format your manuscript (or any document) makes a big difference to how easily and efficiently you will be able to read it, edit it, and look for mistakes.

Text A) This is Times New Roman (10pt), which many people use by default. This font is used in many textbooks, including this one. However, it is generally more difficult to read and edit on a screen. It is even more difficult, if, as in the screenshot on the previous page, there is single line spacing and right-hand justification (red circle in the screenshot below):

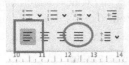

Text B) This is Arial (10 pt). It is has double interlining and is justified to the left only (blue square in the screenshot).

Text C) This is Calibri (12 pt). It is formatted the same as B), but the margins are wider and it is in 12pt. The text thus occupies less space on each line and each word is bigger given the bigger font size. This tends to make it easier to read.

I would suggest using whatever font you find the easiest to read, but always use double space lining, and do not justify to the right (only to the left).

Don't underestimate the importance of this. I guarantee that you will miss some mistakes if you don't print out your paper in a format that is very easy for you to read.

This section also appears in the Presentations book (3.7), as it is also true for writing scripts for presentations.

11.12   Further reading and exercise books

Other books in this series:

How to Prepare and Give an Academic Presentation
Grammar, Usage and Strategies in Academic English

If you want to do exercises in relation to the points covered in this book, then try these three books:

English for Academic Research: Writing Exercises

English for Academic Research: Grammar Exercises

English for Academic Research: Vocabulary Exercises

If you want more details about using English to carry out your research and communicate with others, then the following books from the *English for Academic Research* series are recommended.

English for Academic Research: Grammar, Usage and Style

English for Writing Research Papers

English for Presentations at International Conferences

English for Academic Correspondence

English for Interacting on Campus

Instead, if you are tired of reading formal academic English and just want to have a bit of fun learning and testing your English

Jokes – *have a laugh and improve your English*

Test your personality – *have fun and learn useful phrases*

Wordsearches – *widen your vocabulary in English*

Word games, riddles and logic tests – *tax your brain and boost your English*

And these two are on general English:

Top 50 grammar mistakes in English – *how to avoid them*

Top 50 vocabulary mistakes in English – *how to avoid them*

Good luck with your publication. I hope this books helps you to get your research published and read throughout the world. Let me know: adrian.wallwork@gmail.com

If you are in the UK or EU and need your paper editing: e4ac.com

Teacher's Notes

1 General overview

WHO FOR

- Students of academic English (PhD students, postdocs, undergraduates)
- Teachers of English for Academic Purposes (EAP)

ENGLISH LEVEL

Minimum level: mid to upper-intermediate (CEFR level: B2), but can also be used with advanced students (CEFR levels: C1, C2).

If used as a coursebook, the class can consist of students with different levels of English. However, ideally they should all be at the same point in their university curriculum (e.g. all undergraduates or all first-year PhD students)

TYPE AND COVERAGE

Course on academic English (EAP) and/or self-study guide for students.

The book covers the typical skills to write the various sections of an academic paper for publication in a journal. However, the skills learned can be used not only by PhD students and postdocs, but also by undergraduates to write essays, reports, and theses.

STRUCTURE OF BOOK

After an introductory chapter on the importance of communication in academia, Chapters 2–10 cover the various sections of a paper: Introduction, Methods, Results, Discussion, Conclusions, Abstract. The final chapter (Chapter 11) summarizes the entire book and gives ideas on further exercises for improving on the skills learned in this book.

STRUCTURE OF CHAPTERS 2–9

Each chapter includes a series of discussion questions, followed by the aims of each section, the structure, tenses/style, and models/templates. The chapter ends with some useful phrases and <u>additional</u> writing exercises (there are writing exercises in other sections too).

© The Editor(s) (if applicable) and The Author(s), under exclusive license to
Springer Nature Switzerland AG 2022
A. Wallwork, *Writing an Academic Paper in English*, English for Academic
Research, https://doi.org/10.1007/978-3-030-95615-8

Symbols Used in this Book

 Have discussion or think about.

 Explanation of a rule / guideline.

 An exercise to do.

 Key to the discussion points or exercise.

 Expert tips.

Books in the *English for Research* series where readers can find extra details and/or exercises.

3 Rationale – student focused

The idea of this book and its companion volume on Presentations, is to use as much as possible the students' own work and to refer to their own subject / field of research. This means that I have tried as much as possible to limit the length and number of texts that students have to read (see point 11 below to learn about the types of text that I have used). Also, when they have to learn how to present a methodology and describe and discuss their results, they will either be writing about their own research or research done by others in their fields. This means, for example, that a student in biology, doesn't have to read a text about physics and do a related exercise.

This is far more motivating for students than forcing them to read about and discuss areas that are totally out of their subject area.

This means also that this book is probably quite unlike any textbook on academic writing that you have ever used before.

4 Types of students and English level

This book is primarily intended to teach students how to write a paper for possible publication in an academic journal. This presupposes that the students will be Master's, PhDs or post-grad students. In my experience of teaching international students, most of them have reached at least a mid-upper intermediate level of English (CEFR B2), and many of them will be at a very advanced level. In any case, this book is aimed at all levels above mid intermediate – and such students can all be part of the same class. In fact, many of the skills taught in this book are language independent, they are much more about communication. The guidelines given will often work for the student's native language too.

However, the skills learned in this book are also applicable to undergraduates. For instance, as shown, in the table below, learning to write an abstract requires the same skills as writing a summary.

SECTION OF PAPER	SKILLS APPLICABLE TO UNDERGRADUATES
Abstract	Writing summaries
Introduction	Talking about state-of-the-art when writing undergraduate thesis; paraphrasing from the literature
Methods	Describing tests, protocols, equipment etc
Results and Discussion	Interpreting tables and figures, discussing the meaning of certain findings
Conclusions	Any type of academic assignment (essays, reports, etc) entails writing some concluding remarks

Within the same class you can have students with different levels of English, as long as all of them have at least an intermediate level. However, the class should be homogeneous in terms of the type of students. So it is not advisable to mix under-graduates with postgraduates, and ideally PhD students should all be in the same year.

5 Structure

The book consists of 11 chapters. The first chapter is an introduction to writing papers. The aim is to help students understand what being a researcher involves, and what they need to think about before they actually start writing.

Chapters 2–10 deal with each section in the paper – introduction, review of the literature, methods, results, discussion, conclusion and abstract. Abstracts are dealt with at the end because i) researchers typically write the abstract last, ii) the abstract is one of the most difficult sections to write, so it makes sense to learn the skills from the other sections first. However, as a teacher, if you feel it is best to start with Abstracts, or even Methods (which is generally the easiest section to write), then you are free to do so. Apart from a couple of linked exercises, the chapters are all independent from each other, so you can do them in any order.

The last chapter is a summary of the entire book.

Chapters 2–10 follow a similar structure. First, students think about the specific aim / purpose of a section. This is done by comparing the aim with something non-academic from the student's everyday life. For example, a discussion we may have after watching a movie with friends has many similarities with the Discussion section in a paper (see 6.1). Then, for each section, the following points are analysed (but not always in the same order):

- structure

- tenses

- style (*we* vs passive)

- models – i.e. examples of how a particular section should be written

- typical mistakes

- do's and don'ts

- useful phrases

- additional exercises

The last subsection in each chapter always contains additional exercises. There are also exercises in many of the other subsections too.

Three sections – Introductions, Discussions, and Abstracts – have two chapters dedicated to them. This is because these are the most complex sections to write and so there is a lot more to learn about them.

6 How to approach and teach each chapter –A) undergraduates; B) PhD and postdocs

Let's take Discussions as an example (Chapters 6 and 7).

A

Imagine you are teaching undergraduate students. You need to decide which exercises are most appropriate for someone who is not necessarily preparing a paper for publication. Below is a section by section analysis of the Discussions chapters so that you can understand which ones would be appropriate for undergraduates.

6.1 gets students to think about what a Discussion is. The exercise is fun and should help undergraduates to discuss their own work both with their professor and with their fellow students.

6.2–6.4 regard interpreting and highlighting results, these are important skills for undergraduates studying a scientific subject. These exercises, and other similar exercises in this book, require students to find their own examples of texts by accessing journal websites. Undergraduates may not be used to doing this, so it makes sense for you as the teacher to provide them with suitable sample texts.

6.5 is about distinguishing your results from another author's. This is probably not a key skills for undergraduates and could be skipped.

6.6–6.8 entail talking about the limitations of your research. These, too, could possibly be skipped. However it is VERY important for science students to understand the importance of being transparent about results that do not appear to be in line with what they were hoping to find. So maybe you could just use 6.6.

7.1 and 7.2 show to models of how a Discussion should be written. The exercises are useful for getting students to analyse texts both from a linguistic (vocabulary and grammar) and content point of view. They are thus useful for students who maybe preparing for an examination in academic English (e.g. IELTS).

7.3 is review of tenses, so is definitely useful for all students, whatever their position in the academic hierarchy.

7.4 and 7.5 regard the typical mistakes authors make in journal articles. They can be skipped.

7.6 is on Useful Phrases – these do not need to be taught, but you can refer students to them.

7.7 is the final subsection, and like most final subsections of chapters in this book, it contains exercises. The first one is about removing redundancy, which is a key skill for all students. The other exercises are more for PhD and postgrads, and thus could be skipped.

B

Now let's imagine you are teaching students who need to write a research paper for publication in a journal.

1. As a teacher, you need to be really clear what a Discussion is and its purpose – see Chapter 18 in *English for Writing Research Papers* as well as the Chapters 7–9 on key writing skills that particularly apply to the Discussion.

2. Try reading a few Discussions from academic papers that you can find online. Preferably, choose topics that you have some knowledge of. Try to understand if they are written and constructed well – if so, why? if not, why not?

3. Read through Chapters 6 and 7 of this book, and decide which subsections you feel are the most important, and any that you could skip.

4. Look at the exercises, particularly the ones marked ⬚ or ⬛. These are discussion exercises (both icons mean the same thing), with a series of questions to discuss, which involve students working in pairs or groups. However, if you wish, rather than using them as oral exercises, students can simply write the answers. In any case, I recommend using them as oral exercises in order to create variety in your lessons.

5. Now decide the best order to do your chosen subsections and exercises. Note that most subsections are independent of each other, so you don't have to follow the order presented in the book.

6. To maximize the benefits of your presence in the classroom, try to get students to do any of the longer written exercises at home. So go through the exercises and decide which ones work best in class, and which could be set as homework.

7. Prepare a few notes for your lesson plan and then you're ready to go! Don't worry if you don't follow your lesson plan, let the students' needs, interests and curiosity dictate what you cover.

7 Which sections are useful for undergraduates? Which ones might be suitable for ILETS and similar examinations?

Essentially, all the sections are useful for undergraduates except the very few that regard technical aspects of writing papers for international journals: for example 1.5 regards the' instructions to authors' typically found on journal websites, and which are probably not that important for undergraduates. In any case, as suggested in the previous section, decide which sections would be benefit your students the most rather than indiscriminately doing all the sections in the book.

While this course was not specifically intended for practising the IELTS exam (or similar academic English exams), many of the writing exercises are useful for practising the writing tasks in the exam. However, I would say that to do the exercise effectively, the students really need to be at a university level (so not high school).

8 How long should it take to teach each chapter?

Chapters 2–9 should take 2–4 hours each. The time taken will depend on how experienced you are as an EAP teacher, how many subsections you decide to cover, and how many exercises are set for homework rather than being done in class.

I would say you need a minimum of 20 hours to complete a course. In those 20 hours you will not be able to cover all the points in the book, but certainly the most important ones. However, you could extend it to 30, 40, 60 or even 90 hours if you i) did all the exercises, and ii) combined it with a course on giving presentations: see the companion volume *English for Academic Presentations – Intermediate Level*. In fact, I strongly suggest that you do combine your writing course with a presentations course. Just doing writing alone can be quite heavy for students. There are also many common skills between writing and presenting, so students will have a much clearer and more practical idea of how to implement these skills in a combined course.

9 Vocabulary and useful phrases; useful websites

This book does not have specific vocabulary exercises – such exercises can be found in *English for Academic Research: Vocabulary Exercises*. Instead, the non-technical vocabulary that students will need can be found in the Useful Phrases sections in Chapters 3, 4, 5, 7, 8 and 10. These useful phrases are presented like this:

> *The instrument* used / utilized / adopted / employed *was* …

> *The apparatus* consists of / is made up of / is composed of / is based on …

The words and phrases in normal script show how the same concept can be expressed in a variety of ways. With the Useful Phrases students can learn:

- synonyms
- link words (e.g. those used to show procedures – *first, second, and then, finally*; to interpret and compare: *however, on the other hand*; to show consequences – *thus, therefore* etc.)
- how certain tenses are used in particular ways depending on the section of the paper and point in that section (e.g. use of present perfect in the initial sentences in the Conclusions – see Useful Phrases 29)
- the kind of information that the reader (and reviewers) expect to find in a particular section of the paper

The phrases also act as a template in which students can then insert their own key words, findings and interpretations. There is an index of the Useful Phrases on page 191.

****

I believe it is vital that both teachers and students are aware of websites and applications that can help them during their writing. Here are three sites that I use myself in relation to vocabulary:

https://wikidiff.com/ – explains differences in meaning between words.

context.reverso.net – shows words in context and how they are translated from one language to another (a similar service is offered by linguee.com). The first few pages of returns generally show how a word is typically translated / used, but by scrolling down you can find a lot of alternatives (not necessarily synonyms) to translate the same word, and this will help your students expand their vocabulary and learn often more appropriate words.

https://translate.google.com/ – this application is best NOT for individual words – so students should not type in an individual word and see the translation, but should type in the word in a context. By giving a context, Google Translate stands a much better chance of translating the word correctly.

Clearly, you can also use online dictionaries, but I find the above sites quicker to use and with clearer results.

10 Encouraging students to review each other's work

One exercise at the end of some chapters is for students to analyse the relevant section (e.g. the results section if they are doing the chapter on Results) in a published paper. As an alternative, students could critically analyse each other's papers and then provide feedback. This should encourage them to work together when writing papers – even on different topics. Often we are better at seeing the defects and possible improvements in other people's work rather than our own. Giving feedback is also a key skill for an academic as they are likely to be called on to review a co-author's work, to do peer reviews for journals, or to respond to feedback on their own paper in their rebuttal letter. So if you can teach students how to give diplomatic feedback you will be teaching them a real life skill.

11 A note on the example / model texts

In the previous books that I have written, and in books on scientific writing written by other EAP authors, there is a massive variety of texts from all disciplines. The aim is to provide students with authentic examples.

The downside of this is that every text has new vocabulary and thus <u>comprehension</u> of the text tends to dominate over understanding the <u>purpose</u> of the text and how it is <u>structured</u>.

In this book I opted for a different approach. I wanted the students to be immediately able to understand the text so that they could focus on the exercises, rather than on first wasting time deciphering the meaning. So I have invented some totally fictitious research: the premise of which is that there is a direct relationship between one's level of selfishness and whether one breaks an egg at the big end or small end. The idea of egg breaking, which I hope students will find amusing, is stolen from Swift's *Gulliver's Travels*.

In each chapter there are examples of extracts from papers on this topic. This means that the students only have to understand the key vocabulary once. The key vocabulary includes the following words: *selfish, selfishness, egoism, behavior, queue jumping, litter* (and some other 'selfish' behaviors) and 'endedness', a word that I have coined and which refers to someone's predilection for breaking the egg at one end rather than another. The 'research' makes out that big-enders (BEs) are naturally more selfish than small-enders (SEs).

In any case, the texts are not supposed to be part of the same paper. They are simply on the same topic.

The topic of selfishness did not lend itself to all the points I wished to make, so there are a couple of texts that talk about batteries in cell phones!

12 How this book differs from other EAP books on writing skills

What makes this book truly different from other EAP books is getting students to really understand

- what a research paper is

- what each section is designed to do

- what readers, editors and reviewers expect to see in each section and what they <u>don't</u> need or want to see

- the importance of highlighting THEIR results and differentiating them from OTHER authors' results

- the importance of readability – the aim is not just to get a paper published, but above all to get as many people to read and understand it as possible

Grammar in this book focuses almost exclusively on the tenses required for each section. If your students need extra help with, for example, the use of relative clauses, then they can refer to the companion book *Grammar Usage and Strategy*, and to the exercises in the three exercise books the English for Academic Research series:

English for Academic Research: Writing Exercises

English for Academic Research: Grammar Exercises

English for Academic Research: Vocabulary Exercises

In this book, there is a lot of focus on structuring the sections, which naturally entails structuring sentences and paragraphs. Again, if the students need more practice in these skills, then you can set them exercises from the above three books, and if their level is quite advanced then they can read the relevant chapters in *English for Writing Research Papers*.

My 35-year experience of having a scientific editing agency has taught me that you can have a grammatically perfect paper but it doesn't mean that readers will read it and cite in their papers. I have taught thousands of PhD students how to write their papers. They tend to think that grammar is the key issue, but often totally neglect areas such as redundancy and ambiguity, which are two key reasons why papers are rejected.

Many EAP courses are geared towards getting students to pass EAP type examinations, which by nature tend to focus on what is easy for the board of examiners to mark / score in the quickest and most automatic way possible. Unfortunately, what is tested isn't necessarily the key skills actually required for writing academic texts.

I have tried to make this book easy to adapt (you can theoretically do the chapters in any order) and practical. Thus I have tried to keep it reasonably short and not require students to do endless exercises on aspects that will not radically improve their chances of being published and cited.

The book is designed to be fun. There are lots of discussion exercises – so students are not merely expected to write the whole time but to discuss WHAT they are writing and WHY they are writing it, and HOW this writing impacts on the reader, and also HOW it connects with other aspects of their lives.

Other Books in this Series

If you are interested in learning about EAP teaching in general, then you can read *English for Academic Research: A guide for teachers*. This teacher's book gives you a lot of background information on academia and the importance of publishing papers and presenting research at conferences. It was written <u>before</u> the book you are reading now, so it makes no reference to it.

Like this Writing Papers book, the two books below are also aimed at students with an intermediate level or above.

Giving an Academic Presentation in English: Intermediate Level

Essential English Grammar and Communication Strategies: Intermediate Level

The other books in the 'English for Academic Research' include the following books, which can be integrated into a course on English for Academic Purposes (EAP).

English for Writing Research Papers*

English for Presentations at International Conferences

English for Research: Usage, Style, and Grammar

100 Tips to Avoid Mistakes in Academic Writing and Presenting

English for Academic Research: Writing Exercises

English for Academic Research: Grammar Writing Exercises

English for Academic Research: Vocabulary Writing Exercises

English for Academic Correspondence

English for Interacting on Campus

English for Academic CVs, Resumes, and Online Profiles

For details see: https://www.springer.com/series/13913.

*English for Writing Research Papers in the *English for Academic Research* series published by SpringerNature is more like a manual. It covers several areas that are not covered in the book you are reading now. It includes chapters on: Planning and Preparation (Chapter 1), Structuring a sentence: word order (2), Structuring paragraphs (3), Breaking up long sentences (4), Being concise and removing redundancy (5), Avoiding ambiguity, repetition, and vague language (6), Clarifying who did what (7), Highlighting your findings (8), Discussing your limitations (9), Hedging and criticizing (10), Plagiarism and paraphrasing (11).

If you are an EAP teacher the above chapters will certainly help you understand the process of writing an academic paper.

© The Editor(s) (if applicable) and The Author(s), under exclusive license to
Springer Nature Switzerland AG 2022
A. Wallwork, *Writing an Academic Paper in English*, English for Academic
Research, https://doi.org/10.1007/978-3-030-95615-8

14 Feedback and suggestions

If you have any ideas about how to improve this book, or you have any useful exercises that you think could be integrated, then please let me know.

Despite the text being read multiple times, there will always be a few typos that slip through the net. If you find any, then please email me.

adrian.wallwork@gmail.com

About the Author

Adrian Wallwork is the co-founder of English for Academics (e4ac.com), which specializes in editing and revising scientific papers. Adrian also holds courses on English for Scientific Communication for PhD students. He has written course books for Oxford University Press, discussion books for Cambridge University Press, and other books for BEP and Scholastic and several publishers in Italy. He also self publishes controversial discussion books (tefldiscussions.com).

For SpringerNature, he has written three series of books on Academic English, Business English and General English.

His passion is teaching PhD students and researchers how to write and present their research – see https://e4ac.com/courses

© The Editor(s) (if applicable) and The Author(s), under exclusive license to   187
Springer Nature Switzerland AG 2022
A. Wallwork, *Writing an Academic Paper in English*, English for Academic
Research, https://doi.org/10.1007/978-3-030-95615-8

Acknowledgements

Biggest thanks, as always, to Anna Southern, my unofficial editor. Thanks to Susan Safren at Springer for believing in me and this project.

Huge thanks to all our clients and students at English for Academics (e4ac.com) – without your input this book would never have been possible.

Thanks to The American Veterinary Medical Association for allowing me to reproduce an extract from their instructions to authors.

Finally, thanks to Joaquín Tintoré for sharing his ideas and paper on the new role of scientists in the era of open science.

© The Editor(s) (if applicable) and The Author(s), under exclusive license to
Springer Nature Switzerland AG 2022
A. Wallwork, *Writing an Academic Paper in English*, English for Academic
Research, https://doi.org/10.1007/978-3-030-95615-8

Index of Useful Phrases

Introduction

1 key terminology in your field

2 panorama of past-to-present literature

3 reviewing the literature

4 what specific authors of have stated

5 limitations of previous studies

6 structure of the paper

Methods

7 purpose of testing / methods used

8 apparatus and materials

9 software

10 similarities with, and customizations of, other authors' models, systems etc

11 equations, theories and theorems

12 reasons for choosing your specific method, model, equipment, sample

13 preparation of samples, solutions etc

14 selection procedure for samples, surveys etc

15 time frame of tests (past tenses)

16 time frame in a general process (present tenses)

17 benefits of your method, equipment etc

Results

18 how you got your results

19 tables and figures

20 what you found

21 what you did not find

22 results from questionnaires and interviews

A. Wallwork, *Writing an Academic Paper in English*, English for Academic
Research, https://doi.org/10.1007/978-3-030-95615-8

Discussion

23 referring back to your research aim

24 making transitions, referring to other parts of the paper

25 significant results and achievements

26 opinions and probabilities

27 results in contrast with previous evidence

28 limitations

Conclusions

29 announcing your conclusions and restating the key results

30 highlighting limitations (see also 28)

31 applications and implications of your work

32 future work

33 acknowledgements

Abstracts

34 importance of your topic

35 gap in knowledge and possible limitations

36 aim of your paper and its contribution

37 purpose of testing and methods used

38 what you found

39 benefits of your approach, method, equipment etc

Full Table of Contents

7 Which sections are useful for undergraduates? Which ones might be suitable for ILETS and similar examinations?

8 How long should it take to teach each chapter?

9 Vocabulary and useful phrases; useful websites

10 Encouraging students to review each other's work

11 A note on the example / model texts

12 How this book differs from other EAP books on writing skills

13 Other books in this series

14 Feedback and suggestions

Index by Section